Imagining Movement

An exploration of Mental Imagery

and

An extensive review of sports-based,
mental imagery-related literature

Benjamin Samples

Copyright © 2017 SCB Press

First edition.

All rights reserved.

ISBN: 0981760031
ISBN-13: 978-0-9817600-3-2

TO SVETOCHKA

ever hopeful, ever positive, and ever moving

CONTENTS

	Acknowledgments	i
1	Seeking Thrills	1
2	On the Move	6
3	A Philosophy of Movement	11
4	Three Spheres	17
5	Chair Flying	26
	References	35
	Related Literature Review	39

ACKNOWLEDGMENTS

Many thanks to my fellow learners and thrill seekers!

1 SEEKING THRILLS

About a century ago, philosopher William James theorized (James et al, 1979):

> "It is only by risking our persons from one hour to another that we live at all. And often enough our faith beforehand in an uncertified result is the only thing that makes the result come true."

Temple Psychologist Frank Farley characterized the United States as a "Type T" Nation—a personality dimension referring to stimulation seeking, excitement seeking, thrill (T) seeking, arousal seeking, and risk taking (Morchouse, 1990; Farley, 1986).

Perhaps more so than in any other segment of society, this need for a thrill has solidified its presence in the evolving world of sports and performance, as chronicled over a decade ago in the US News & World Report article, "Extreeeme" [sic] (Koerner, 1997). Spread across the cover of the magazine, the following words still resonate with today's sporting public: "Extreme Sports: Why Americans are risking life and limb for the big rush."

This article and numerous other works point to socio-cultural, genetic, economic, even racial constructs to understand the phenomenon of extreme sports and their impact on American sport culture (Booth & Thorpe, 2007; King et al, 2007; Coakley & Dunning, 2000).

While there is still disagreement among the sport community as to what to call these activities—extreme sports, alternative sports, whiz sports, lifestyle sports, or even panic sports (Coakley & Dunning, 2000)—or even what activities are included—such as ski-BASE jumping, steep skiing, white water kayaking, stunt/freestyle biking, skateboarding, etc. (Rinehart & Sydnor, 2003)—Farley maintains that this Type T behavior stands as a very constructive function that empowers human creativity and ingenuity. He reveals, "I believe that whenever you see human progress, you are going to see a big T standing there. You know these are the people who change the world ... Albert Einstein" (Farley, 2011).

Extreme sports obviously include a strong risk element, but as a developing phenomenon continually advancing to new levels, it includes components of originality and inventiveness: such physical demonstration of skill is not simply about risk, but also artistic, creative presentation.

Matthias Giraud mixes avalanches, big mountain skiing, and BASE jumping at Aiguille Croche in Megeve France. Giraud's first well-known ski-BASE jump was off the Mississippi Head on Mt Hood in Oregon State. Photo Courtesy of Loveskiing Team, circle added to emphasize Mr. Giraud beneath the canopy of his parachute.

This same expression is found throughout the world of movement and performance, be it in traditional team sports like baseball, body awareness activities like hand-standing or yoga, and even activities ranging from biking to powerlifting to aerobatics. While participants develop, succeed, fail, and try again, they put in the balance their faith in anticipated outcomes and the thrill of avoiding unanticipated ones.

As faith transitions to physical capability, the thrill shifts from failure avoidance to advanced proficiency and achieved competency; this is a place where movement becomes as much a spiritual activity as it is a realistic activity.

It is where amazing things happen.

An examination not of Why, but How

Anecdotally, researchers seem to be actively exploring the cognitive dimensions associated with "Why" individuals participate in these types of risky activities; in light of Dr. James' theorizing, it is also valuable to consider "How" individuals participate in these activities so that their successes rest in more than "faith" alone.

What are the physical, cognitive, and social processes that allow athletes—both novice and expert—to accomplish new maneuvers or perform known skills? Of particular interest, how do they interact with their sports' operational environments to execute such complex tasks, especially when failure includes the very real risk of bodily harm; and furthermore, how can you develop this cognitive and behavioral mentality to augment your sport environment and it's associated technologies to enhance your athletic experience?

This book specifically examines the realm of visualization and mental imagery as it applies to movement and performance and provides a fairly extensive literature review for those interested in delving a little deeper into the minutiae of relevant research.

2 ON THE MOVE

Movement.

It's the essence of what separates us from the inanimate world of the dead. The beauty of physical performance is so multi-faceted. It is evidenced in the grace of a dancer, the coordination of a baseball player, the press of a powerlifter, the agility of a gymnast, the inputs of an aerobatic pilot, and a number of other characteristics present to varying degrees in a multitude of activities. For the professional it looks so fluid, calculated, and natural.

Without a doubt, I can say I've been truly blessed with a life full of adventure. And through it, movement has proven my passion. I am incessantly active and stay eternally busy, pushing the envelope both physically and mentally.

Probably my first real "sport" was baseball, but I

was as often to be found on a bmx bike as with a baseball glove. I was always the youngest kid on the team, contending against the older players, and often rising to the top. I was always the first one over the bike ramp or to try to clear a gap or try a new trick (and admittedly, the first one to bite the dirt). I continually thirst for progression.

As a teenager, I was already active in rock climbing, kayaking, skiing, swimming and other activities. During my undergraduate studies, I began racing motorcycles and ice climbing. After graduation, I joined up with the Army's 19th Special Forces Group (Airborne), where I learned to operate in dangerous tactical environments with the utmost precision.

This is also where my interests in weightlifting were first piqued. A few years later, I started working with fitness clients as a trainer while doing contract work. I first certified as an NSCA CSCS and as an NSCA-CPT not long after.

Later, during my master's studies, as if to come full circle, I rediscovered my love for biking and got really serious with downhill mountain biking and dirt jumping. Since then, in addition to training and managing fitness clients, I've been flying airplanes and helicopters, and most recently exploring aerobatics as my thrill of choice.

A trip to the pool
At a very young age, before I ever picked up a

baseball or rode a mountain bike, I learned the inseparable relationship between mental imagery and movement.

Along with the other neighborhood kids, and well before injury lawsuits ran so rampant, we spent summers at the community pool which boasted three diving boards, one of which was at least 15 feet high. I remember the sound of that spring board clanging and bouncing all through the summer. For some, the goal was a huge splash that would reach the girls sunbathing along the side of the pool. For others, it was a perfect dive with the slightest slurp of a splash.

For me it was aerobatic.

What kind of flip, twist, or movement could I make in the weightlessness of space before I was brought back down to the reality of the water below?

I remember mimicking and trying to one-up my buddies. At first, I could flip way better than I could twist, then I'd try combinations. The forward-facing back flip (the half "gainer") was my true nemesis. There was a fear of the dreaded back-buster: a quarter flip that ended in a back-first water landing and coming out red-skinned and in pain. Even worse was the thought of the Louganis: slamming the back of your head on the rebounding board and being carried out of the pool bloodied and beaten.

I had experienced both.

My buddy had the trick totally tuned in though. You could see him standing on the side of the pool with his eyes shut going through motions with his hands and head. Some would chuckle at him on their way by. One day he mentored me through the movements. "Shut your eyes Ben;" "First, a nice large spring, your head looking skyward as your core contracts, bringing your knees toward your chest. After you see horizon, then you see your spot in the water. Unloading, body extending, arms outstretched, halting rotation, and then splash!"

I could see it so clearly, every aspect in detail felt so real. For the moment though, it was still simply a concept. I imagined my way through it several more times, then it was go-time. With a little bravado and a lot of trepidation, I climbed the ladder and headed out toward the end of the spring board. The movements felt so routine, so natural. Splash! It had to have been a beautiful dive!

As I emerged from the water, it was like a baptism. I was different. A few minutes ago I had never successfully performed the gainer, and now it was reality.

I began to notice the value of this mental connection to movement throughout everything I did in life. Visualization was a form of mental exercise that strengthened my faith in some desired outcome.

But it was more than that.

I could see the moves I'd make to climb some cliff in front of me. I could try out scenarios in my mind. A certain sequence of moves might make sense at the bottom of the rock but set you up for failure further up. I could fix these errors in my mind well before my hands ever touched stone. The imagining of the activity grew ever stronger, increasingly integrating all the senses into a internally realistic world of possibility.

3 A PHILOSOPHY OF MOVEMENT

In addition to being a fitness professional with the National Strength and Conditioning Association (NSCA), I was also a design researcher at the University of Washington. I studied how people attain expertise and progress from the state of a novice to that of a professional.

I want you to begin thinking about how you, yourself, are becoming an expert in the tasks you put your mind to.

While some academic researchers examine this progression through knowledge in terms of people becoming an expert in more traditionally mental domains (like mathematics or engineering or accounting), my interests are more concerned with how people become expert in "physiocognitive" domains.

This is the world of sports and movement.

"Physio" refers to the physical nature of actions: catching a baseball out in centerfield, flipping a bicycle through the air, landing a round-off back handspring, spiking a volleyball, piloting an airplane through stall recovery, and so on.

"Cognitive" refers to the mental processes that empower these actions: mental imagery, forecasting, reviewing, etc.

Think about how different it is to be the professional engineer who designs an airplane versus the expert pilot who steers it through aerobatic maneuvers, risking life and limb, making numerous decisions every second and providing physical inputs to alter her physical reality continually throughout the activity. Moreover, consider the baseball outfielder who sees a ball come off the bat, takes off running across the field, blocks the sun with his glove and meets the ball's trajectory just at the right time before tossing it over it over a hundred feet back to the pitcher with the accuracy of a sniper.

Such physiocognitive actions are so amazing; the processing power involved is probably far greater than we'd ever see in any robotic design lab.

Nevertheless, think of how different these levels of expertise are from becoming an expert in math or science.

When we consider sports and movement, it seems we are oft times more concentrated on the physical side of things and let the cognitive side fall away. Keep in mind however, that every movement we make starts with cognition and the firing of neurons in our brains.

The physiocognitive domain is best understood through an embodied approach that emphasizes the strong connection between form and function. If you place a table in the foyer of your home, what happens to it after a week or so? Things start piling up, right? First it's the house keys. Then sunglasses. Then those keys that you are not sure what they go to. Then the phone, maybe some spare change, your watch... but you see what's happening. A table holds an inherent attraction for our need to place things on it. There is a strong connection between the physical characteristics of an object and the actions and activities that surround the object. Soviet-era psychologists first distinguished this relationship in what Alexei Nikolaevich Leont'ev called Activity Theory.

Such ideas have also found their way into many other domains, even into the practice of osteopathy and osteopathic medicine, founded by physician Andrew Taylor Still.

Our bodies are truly remarkable.

From a mechanical perspective, we might be a collection of levers, moment arms, and pumps. From an electrical perspective, we are a network of switches, transistors, and intricate wiring. From a chemical perspective, a psychological perspective, a religious perspective... I could go on and on. The form of our bodies—the way we are built, the way these levers move, our muscles pump, and our nerves fire—this form determines the way we move and the way we take our selves to ever higher levels of functioning.

Moreover, this functioning is further enhanced by the machines and technologies we utilize to complete our movements. For some activities, it may be a ball, for others it's a bar and weight, for others it's a bicycle, a kayak, a springboard, or even an airplane! It's simply amazing to get a little metaphysical for a few moments and consider all the wonder we see in the simple movements we make each day.

So why all this psychobabble about physio-cognitive domains, embodied approaches, and activity theory? Aren't we just moving around and playing with cool toys?

Because when you get the results you want, it will not be the product of some simple set of steps that you go through. It won't be by chance. It will be the commitment to a mindset that develops your movement goals.

Everything we do—our jobs, our relationships, our activities, our movements, everything—begins with the mind.

This is particularly true in our sport and movement goals. You need to know what's going on and take productive initiative to realize your goals. Success begins with determining what exactly is required to be successful. Then you have to figure out how to accomplish these prerequisite inputs.

To make something happen, you need to

Imagining Movement

understand what it is you want to make happen and what you have to do to make it happen.

Our bodies, as amazing as they are, are simply the objects and actions of our minds. While our bodies and the movements we make with them are bound by their structure, our minds continually reshape our capabilities and elevate our potentials. Everywhere—in life, in love, at work, in the gym, on the playing field, out in the wild, everywhere—we will begin to see that the results we want are first conceived, constructed, and confirmed in the realm of the mind.

You will hear me talk less and less about a sport and more and more about movement and imagination. We are not concerned with a particular "state" or an "event;" these pass in an instant and simply become memories of what "was." We are interested in activity—what "is" and what "ought to be."

As "thinking" beings, we perceive the world around us. We take in millions upon millions of precepts based on what we see, smell, feel, taste, and hear. We develop these sensory inputs into some understanding of how the world "is." We analyze, compare, hypothesize, and reanalyze. We design procedures, evaluate alternatives, process outcomes, and then, a spark of magic occurs. Instead of simply reacting or observing, we impose action. We uniquely reshape our conceptual understanding of the world around us from what "is" to what "ought to be."

Based on our perspective of the mechanics of

nature (and often our tolerance of risk) we attempt to concretize our unique concept into a planned, purposeful realization.

What once was simply a "possible" outcome is now reality.

It is concrete, observable, tacit.

It is real.

This action, this confirmation and realization of some concept, quite often becomes the "something" that those around us perceive, and the cycle continues. It is our actions that essentially define us as dynamic living beings.

Out of what "is," we shape the world around us according to what we believe it can be.

4 THREE SPHERES

I should make note that an idea of "imagining movement," while related, is still quite separated from visualizing a successful life or the "power of positive thinking." Likewise is it also separate from and does not replace quality practice and successful competitive exposure.

Nevertheless, imagining movement—the mental visualization associated with it—is a form of learning, reviewing, and actual practice.

In performance, there should obviously be much interest in controlling our muscles and their contractions. In the Essentials of Strength Training and Conditioning, Baechle and Earle define mental imagery as "a cognitive physiological skill in which the athlete uses all the senses to create a mental experience of an athletic performance." They go on to describe progression of the skill where the imagery gets clearer and clearer with practice.

With my clients at the gym, I constantly remind them, "there's nothing gained in lifting the weights, they are only there to make our muscles contract." We need be interested in establishing a mental connection between the movements that our mind considers and the actual movement that our muscles make.

Just like the weights, your legs or arms or feet have no inherent reason to move out into some position; movements are about body awareness, functionality, and ultimately, performance.

Mental imaging encompasses all the senses and is traditionally broken down into a few spheres of practice: **external**, **internal**, and **kinesthetic**.

The external sphere is essentially viewing some activity from outside of your body. This perspective is well suited to working collaboratively with other individuals where you can watch a performance. The internal sphere gives you a first-person perspective, preparing you for the sight-pictures and sounds of your activity. The kinesthetic sphere embodies mental imagery, linking muscles, bones, and joints into a connected whole, ready for action. There is overlap, and obviously each sphere might be more suited to particular parts of a given activity or to different levels of advancement.

Out of the abyss
While living in the Pacific North West, I probably

Pacific northwest rider, Lucas Chalcraft (of GHY Cycles in Renton, Washington), wows riding friends in Washington State. This is one of hundreds of similar trails around Seattle, WA. Photo courtesy of Walter Yi (2011).

spent more time on two wheels than on my own two feet. My academic research was situated around environmental interaction and expertise development in extreme sports, and what better place to explore such behaviors than at a bike park.

Our favorite dirt jump spot was Duthie Hill, a bike park situated just out side of town that was sanctioned by the Evergreen Mountain Bike Association with at least a partial purpose of making you a better rider. It has numerous skills sections that allow progression through larger and larger jumps and other components that support your progression from novice thru expert. There are balance-beam styled features, teeter-totters, drops, berms, flow parks, slalom courses, everything you could imagine!

One jump in particular is a giant step-up ramp. A 15-foot-tall wooden tower stands out in the woods, tempting those who dare to climb its stairs. Off the opposite side is a steep descent, like dropping into a deep quarter pipe.

Beyond the tower, the contour of the land continues the steep decline another 20 feet into what might more appropriately be called a deep abyss. At this point you're cruising along nearly 30 miles an hour. After pumping over a little roller feature to load up the bike, you're hurled up a 12-foot-tall ramp that is nearly vertical at the top.

Lift off!

You fly another 10-12 feet into the air, topping out in a weightless state of euphoria before realizing "what goes up, must come down!" The landing zone is somewhat sloped to slow your descent and super sandy to provide some amount of cushion should your attempt at flight go awry.

This particular jump has seen its share of many bent bike parts, a multitude of bloodied shins, a number of broken bones, and occasionally, absolute aerial artistry. In my early thirties, I was definitely an old guy. My heroes and mentors were 16-year-olds with nothing to lose.

But I had everything to gain.

My first goal was to cleanly land a big air 360 from the giant step-up ramp. I had seen only three, maybe four of the hundreds of other riders at the park routinely land the maneuver.

An external sphere

At first I could only watch the others perform the 360. If I was lucky, someone was there and trying it when I happened to be there. When it worked for them, it was so smooth and fluid. I would ask how they learned to do the trick and most couldn't really put it into words. "I just kept trying, one day it clicked."

But what did it mean to "try?"

I videoed a couple guys successfully nailing the 360. I set up my camera from the top of the tower, from down in the abyss, from just beyond the landing area, every angle I could think of. I went home and reviewed on the big screen. I could see the inputs: loading and unloading with the legs off the top of the ramp, leading with the head and eyes, core movements, positioning for and absorbing the landing.

What I noticed though, is that when I turned off the television, I could still imagine each of those inputs as if I were watching them from their respective filming locations. I could even see my future self doing the maneuver from each of those viewpoints.

This is the realm of the external sphere of mental imagery perspectives.

When I watch the 360 happening from outside of

my body I am able to see the big picture from different vantage points while zoning in on the specific, practical aspects of the maneuver.

When do I leave the ramp? What is my trajectory? How does the movement unfold throughout the trajectory? How is the transition to landing made?

Throughout the following days I could see my self turning through the 360 and successfully landing it every time.

An internal sphere

Back at the park, I was ready to give it a try.

I climbed the tower and looked out from the perspective that I had played out in my head no less than a few hundred times, and off I went. Rolling down the steep decline, over the roller, and up the ramp: lift off!

About half way through the turn I had no idea where I was.

I'm not sure if I shut my eyes or what, but I know I had this blurry glance of sand and dirt coming at me in a hurry. I had already ejected my bike and was bracing for impact.

Not too painful actually. A little dirty, bike's in fine shape, though.

When I got up and gathered my senses, I realized something. Once I was airborne, looking down into the abyss of the roller area was quite frightening as I spun around some 15-20 feet in the air. I had never noticed that from all the viewpoints I had watched over and over.

I decided to find a nice spot to lie down there in the woods by the Duthie Hill step-up and take a first-person, mental imagery trip throughout this 360-degree maneuver. From the top of the tower, I looked down through the decline and through the natural contours of the run-up area. As I ascended the actual ramp, the trees rose out of the forest in front of me. Topping the ramp my eyes began leading to the right and as my head turned, I was looking behind me, down deep into the abyss. It was only temporary though. As my head continued to spin, my body followed suit. In an instant I could spot my landing area. Success!

This is the realm of the internal sphere of mental imagery perspectives.

I was watching the 360 happening from inside my body, from own viewpoint, realizing the pictures and sights that would flash through my eyes, discounting and preparing for the surprises that may take me off guard as I successfully spin through the air.

Over the next week or so, I went back and forth imagining the maneuver from both the external and internal spheres, keying in on the particular aspects that were going to make this stunt work.

A kinesthetic sphere

My next series of trips to the step-up were brutal!

Attempt after attempt proved unsuccessful. Perfect trajectory destroyed by a lack of leading with my head and eyes, a complete 360 while totally missing the landing slope, ejection after ejection! Sweaty clothes filled with sand, bloodied shins, and bruised pride.

Time for a break.

I sat there at the top of the tower, wishing I could hop in a nice cool pool like I always had as a child. Then I remembered the gainer from the spring board.

The motions.

The movements.

I stood up on the tower and shut my eyes. My hands reached out in front of me as if gripping the handlebars of my bike. While internally visualizing the movements of cruising down into the abyss, over the roller, and up the step-up, I literally mimicked each action with my body. I could feel the wind in my face, I could even smell the evergreen pines. The pump, the lift-off, I could hear the friction of my wheels leaving the earth. Turning my head, I could see the abyss behind me. I turned my body, leading with my head, feeling the stretch and then contraction in my core while imagining the landing spot coming into view. As my body rotated, I could feel the weight and flow of the bike underneath me. As I set up for landing my legs began to tense in expectation of a perfectly balanced landing. My arms reached out slightly to level and absorb the landing.

360 degrees later, I opened my eyes and saw the ramp out in the distance beyond the abyss below me.

I had just connected the visual imagery to the physical sensations.

Let's do this!

Down the decline I went. Through the abyss. Up the ramp, launching, spinning, flying!

As my wheels landed in the dirt, I knew it had to have been beautiful. As I stepped off my bike, it was, once again, like a baptism. A little more sweaty and dirty than I ever was at the pool, but still I was different. A few minutes ago I had never successfully performed the 360, and now it was reality.

This is the realm of the kinesthetic sphere of mental imagery perspectives.

When I match the internal imagery of the 360 with the realistic external bodily movements, I am essentially executing the maneuver. The only difference is that on the ramp, the movements are happening in a dynamic, consequential space, whereas my kinesthetic visualization is simply happening in a small, static, experimental area with no consequences and 100% success.

5 CHAIR FLYING

Research in the area of sports yields novel insights into human behavior and learning. Mental imagery is normally situated in a pre-activity sequence of events. It is often simply touted as a way to prepare for action. Nevertheless, it is equally impactful as a review technique. Error-spotting and fine-tuning through visualization is very powerful.

Perhaps the most overlooked characteristic of mental imaging, though, is engaging in it DURING performance.

Many athletes seem to disappear into a "zone" during performance: a sort of hybrid of actuality and some imagined reality where they can essentially navigate through a perfectly forecasted series of events in pure movement artistry.

As sports get more and more extreme, the necessity of being ahead of your game is paramount.

But even in traditional sports, athletes develop mental, visualized schemas that enhance their actions.

There is actually a biological connection.

Roure et al (1998) illustrated that mental rehearsal of activities and movements literally activated beneficial responses from the autonomic nervous system. This means that visualization is not just a spacey mental concept, it is a chemical reaction that enhances performance. Studies have shown that virtual workouts yield calculable results. Dryw Dworsky, Ph.D. & Vikki Krane, Ph.D. of Bowling Green State University even postulate that mental imagery can benefit healing and recovery.

Through situational analysis, researchers are examining how aerial freestyle skiers land on their feet after flipping and twisting numerous times over 60 feet in the air (Hauw & Durand, 2007). Olympic ski jumpers regularly participate in an imagining of their aerial movements. Watching videos of this activity, you can realize that it is a true, physical practice: the athletes finish a few minutes of imagery and kinesthetic visualization and are physically exhausted.

Other work is exploring how elite trampolinists understand and perform their skills (Hauw & Durand, 2007). As represented in numerous other articles, embodied, spatially-oriented interactions in high risk environments represent a very transdisciplined-topic spanning Human Factors, Cognitive Science, Information Design, Sport Psychology, and more. Though prior research has examined human factors in risky situations, there seems to be limited research exploring how purposefully-advanced mental imaging and perceptual functions support the development and performance of advanced physical capabilities in high-risk environments—beyond primarily cognitive abilities. Hopefully, academia will follow suit.

Semantics, syntactics, and pragmatics

In my specialty, Human Centered Design and Engineering, there is a degree of removed-ness from the purely physical environment. To a certain extent, our research deals with cerebral abstractions, disembodied from corporeal interactions.

Consider designing for a complex train navigation system versus a business management system: each requires many of the same inputs and both have important outcomes and valuable results to explore.

But is there something dissimilar between designing for corporeal 8,000 tons of train travelling 60 mph through busy cities and the more purely cerebral interactions of 8,000 employees distributed across 60 cities speaking different languages?

The further technology separates us from directly operating in and interacting with an objective, tangible reality, the stronger our semantic, syntactic, and pragmatic understandings of our reality must become: a deeper semantic understanding implying a sturdier relationship between what we see in the wild and what it means to us; a greater syntactic understanding entailing a firmer connection amongst the words and thoughts we use to comprehend what we see; and a superior pragmatic understanding relating to the biological and psychosocial processes we use to interact with what we see.

These are the themes with which we begin to advance our ability to visualize and imagine.

Seeing better

As we navigate our way through our activity's process or system, we are basically participating in a form of communication with that system (Jesus, 1994).

Think about something as simple as the interstate system and driving your car from one location to another. On a macro level, you develop a sort of mental imagery that directs you along your route and helps you prepare for a particular exit. On a micro level, you may imagine how your vehicle speeds up or slows down in time to change lanes and fit in front of the semi truck before your exit.

As the danger of our process increases, as is often the case with various sports or activities, this communication is vital to our safe and successful completion of the steps involved.

During our daily environmental interactions, we consume visual information almost continually; it provides us directions, additional context, or even warnings. Traditional wayfinding involves the human movement through a constructed environment using natural skills and innate abilities, that is, learning to imagine a system and operate within it (Golledge, 1999). Consider walking through your house in the dark. You may not simply walk until you hit a wall, but instead you have a picture and a layout in your head and instantaneously envision your steps through out the mental image.

Nevertheless, during instances of real-time decision-making in risky environments, our movement may be made more difficult by unfamiliarities within a given system or by the physical layout of the system (Baskaya, et al. 2004). Imagine a firefighter busting through the front door of a burning house and attempting to find the stranded homeowners.

In high-risk activities, poor understanding of visual information can have severe consequences and requires special applications of wayfinding, or "wayshowing," as it is sometimes described from a designer's perspective (Mollerup, 2005).

This fact is certainly pertinent while learning or performing activities requiring the primarily cognitive skills like piloting an aircraft or ship; however, it is also especially relevant to activities that also require high levels of embodied physical skill such as participating in sport performance. It may even be applicable to tactical response operations like S.W.A.T. team raids or military operations.

In these instances, the failure of individuals to maintain spatial awareness as they aggressively make their way through a constructed environment can have harmful consequences for beginners and experts alike.

"Wayshowing" benefits from affordances and mechanisms built into the constructed environment that relay information about how to function in that system; examples include anything from signage and labeling systems, to ecological design considerations, or even associated usage constructs. These mechanisms—which could be described as "experiential context cues"—can act as sorts of cognitive prostheses that relay instruction, direct physical human behaviors, and guide individuals through complex environments and toward increased competencies in high-risk, aggressive activities involving consequential maneuvers.

The more we can interact with and notice the minutiae of our operational environment, the better we can imagine. With experiential context cues, we can purpose the mental imagery of our sporting environment to enhance our spatial cognition and physical interactions resulting in safer and more effective skill development.

We can practice imagining.

It is a skill that can be advanced.

To the extent that we improve our ability to imagine our movements, their requisite inputs and outcomes, we can advance in our performance of complex actions.

Chair flying

Flying light aircraft is very much an exercise in imagining. Physical movements must be small, precise, and exacting: the right amount of stick or rudder, right at the proper moment.

These movements are perfectly informed by mental imagery.

We deal with emergency procedures, startle response suppression, real-time decision making, and a multitude of other concepts.

Slow is smooth and smooth is fast.

Student pilots ask me all the time, "which simulator should I get?"

Granted, a flight simulator has an amazing ability to expose pilots to situations they may never see in flight. But perhaps most valuable (and certainly cheapest) is the simulator in each of our brains. I regularly print off a picture of the dash of their aircraft and tell them to tape it to the wall and find a chair to sit in front of it.

I still do it.

When I first started, it was more about switchology, or where switches were located, when to flip them, and when to make certain inputs. But nowadays, when I chair fly, I have tried to enhance mere visualization with sharper mental imaging.

When I make this turn, do I feel an acceleration? Why do I feel this small yawing motion? What happens to my sight picture? What do I hear near stall?

Watch (not just listen to) any fighter pilot talk about flying aggressive dog-fighting maneuvers. Their hands role-play each aircraft rolling, turning, banking, and climbing. Each movement is augmented verbally by the required control inputs or certain aerodynamic or performance considerations. They will talk through the bodily reaction to excessive Gs while noting the angle of attack of wind flowing over the shuddering wings of the aircraft. There is a conceptual synergy developed between the pilot's mind, body, and machine.

The majority of us will get few opportunities to sit in an Extra 300 aerobatic flying machine, and even fewer will ever sit in an F16, but the techniques of mental imagery and visualization that would make us good at an aileron roll or evasive maneuvers are the same techniques that would help us nail the 360 on our bike, press through our next bench press, or perfect a double gainer from the spring board.

Shut your eyes a little

Before your next trip to the gym, or before you take off on your bicycle, or before you meet up with your buddies for your next basket ball game, take a few minutes and ingest some of the motions you are going to make.

While there is nothing more powerful than quality practice and successful competitive exposure, mental imaging is a potent determiner of your future progression. Baechle and Earle detail that mental imagery provides an environment for certain and repeated success, two potent ingredients in any athlete's performance repertoire.

Start with basic, external mental pictures of your performance.

See them from a distance, move closer.

Step closer, see the movements first-person.

Begin to see movement, identify the specifics of your actions.

Attempt to clarify the visual actions as you bring in the full spectrum of senses: touch, taste, hear, and smell.

Move through the motions as prepare for action.

Elevate your movements to the next level.

REFERENCES

Baechle, T. R., & Earle, R. W. (2008). *Essentials of Strength Training and Conditioning.* Human Kinetics.

Baskaya, A., Wilson, C., & Ozcan, Y. Z. (November 01, 2004). Wayfinding in an unfamiliar environment. *Environment & Behavior,* 36, 6.

Booth, D., & Thorpe, H. (2007). *Berkshire encyclopedia of extreme sports.* Great Barrington, Mass: Berkshire Pub. Group.

Centre for Evidence-Based Conservation. (2010). Guidelines for Systematic Review in Environmental Management. Version 4.0. *Environmental Evidence.* Retrieved 07:50, March 10, 2013, from www.environmentalevidence.org/Authors.htm

Coakley, J. J., & Dunning, E. (2000). *Handbook of sports studies.* London: SAGE.

Farley, F. (May 01, 1986). The Big T in Personality. *Psychology Today,* 20(5), 44-52.

Farley, F. (May 02, 2011). Type T personalities: Thrill-seekers, risk-takers, and rule-breakers. *About Kids Health.* Video retrieved from http://www.aboutkidshealth.ca/

Golledge, R. G. (1999). *Wayfinding behavior: Cognitive mapping and other spatial processes.* Baltimore: Johns Hopkins University Press.

Hauw, D., & Durand, M. (January 01, 2007). Situated analysis of elite trampolinists' problems in competition using retrospective interviews. *Journal of Sports Sciences, 25,*2, 173-183.

Hauw, D., Renault, G., & Durand, M. (September 01, 2008). How do aerial freestyler skiers land on their feet? A situated analysis of athletes' activity related to new forms of acrobatic performance. *Journal of Science and Medicine in Sport, 11,* 5, 481-486.

Helal, A. & Mann, W. (2006). *Promoting Independence for Older Persons with Disabilities: Selected Papers from the 2006 International Conference on Aging, Disability and Independence: Volume 18 Assistive Technology Research Series.* IOS Press.

James, W., Burkhardt, F., Bowers, F., & Skrupskelis, I. K. (1979). *The will to believe and other essays in popular philosophy.* Cambridge, Mass: Harvard University Press.

Jesus, S. C. (December 07, 1994). Environmental communication: design planning for wayfinding. *Design Issues,* 10, 32-51.

King, C., Leonard, D., & Kusz, K. (February 01, 2007). White Power and Sport. *Journal of Sport & Social Issues,* 31, 1, 3-10.

Koerner, B. I. (1997). Extreeeme. (Cover story). *U.S. News & World Report*, 122(25), 50.

Loveskiing Team. (2011). Retrieved on March 20, 2013 (converted to b&w) from:
http://www.loveskiing.co.uk/wp-content/uploads/2011/11/Matthias-Giraud-ski-BASE-jump.jpg

Mollerup, P. (2005). *Wayshowing: A guide to environmental signage; principles & practices*. Baden: Lars Muller.

Morehouse, R. E., Farley, F., & Youngquist, J. V. (1990). Type T Personality and the Jungian Classification System. *Journal Of Personality Assessment*, 54(1/2), 231-235.

Mountain biking in British Columbia. (2012, October 21). In *Wikipedia, The Free Encyclopedia*. Retrieved 06:47, March 9, 2013, from
http://en.wikipedia.org/w/index.php?title=Mountain_biking_in_British_Columbia&oldid=518954825

Mountain biking. (2013, March 8). In *Wikipedia, The Free Encyclopedia*. Retrieved 06:50, March 9, 2013, from
http://en.wikipedia.org/w/index.php?title=Mountain_biking&oldid=542878130

Phibbs, P., & Bridge C. (2003). Protocol guidelines for systematic reviews of home modification information to inform best practice. The University of Sydney Faculties of Health Sciences and Architecture.

Rinehart, R. E., & Sydnor, S. (2003). *To the extreme: Alternative sports, inside and out*. Albany: State University of New York Press.

Roure, R., et al. (1998). Autonomic Nervous System

Responses Correlate with Mental Rehearsal in Volleyball Training. Journal of Applied Physiology, 78(2), 99-108.

Yi, W. (2011). Retrieved on March 20, 2013 (converted to b&w) from:
http://gp1.pinkbike.org/p4pb6021529/p4pb6021529.jpg.

RELATED LITERATURE REVIEW

ATHLETES, EMBODIED COGNITION
Embodiment of motor skills when observing expert and novice athletes
Sinnett, S., Hodges, N. J., Chua, R., & Kingstone, A. (January 01, 2011).
Embodiment of motor skills when observing expert and novice athletes. *Quarterly Journal of Experimental Psychology (2006), 64,* 4, 657-68.

If people are shown a dynamic movie of an action such as kicking a soccer ball or hitting a tennis ball, they will respond to it faster if it requires the same effector. This standard congruency effect was reported to reverse when participants viewed static images of famous athletes not actually performing an action. It was suggested that the congruent response was inhibited because of a social contrast effect, based on an implied action, whereby responders viewed themselves as comparatively worse than the professional athlete. The present study recorded hand and foot responses when identifying static images of both famous and novice athletes in soccer and tennis. The action was either explicit or implied. In Experiment 1, a standard congruency effect was found for all images. In Experiment 2, when a response was based on the identity of the athlete rather than their expertise, the standard congruency effect was enhanced for images of novice athletes, but was eliminated for experts, suggesting a social contrast effect. Our study is the first to show that embodiment effects can be seen for implied and explicit action images of both novices and experts, and that static images are capable of eliciting priming effects associated with sport-relevant effector pairings.

Motor expertise modulates movement processing in working memory
Moreau, D. (March 01, 2013). Motor expertise modulates movement processing in working memory. *Acta Psychologica, 142,* 3, 356-361.

A substantial amount of literature has demonstrated individuals' tendency to code verbally a series of movements for subsequent recall. However, the mechanisms underlying movement encoding remain unclear. In this paper, I argue that sensorimotor expertise influences the involvement of motor processes to store movements in working memory. Experts in motor activities and individuals with limited motor expertise were compared in three experimental conditions assessing movement recall: (a) without suppression task, (b) with verbal suppression, and (c) with motor...

Confronting the Problem of Embodiment
Cheville, J. (January 01, 2005). Confronting the Problem of Embodiment. *International Journal of Qualitative Studies in Education, 18*, 1, 85-107.

Embodiment has become an important construct for those in disciplines and specialty areas concerned with the form and function of the human body. This article suggests that accounts of embodiment have collapsed into an exclusionary framework that locates culture and cognition on oppositional terms. For some scholars, embodiment represents the performance of one's body with cultural contexts that sanction particular forms of comportment and display. Others attend to the neurological or cognitive functions that arise from bodily activity. After a historical analysis that documents how these exclusionary constructs have gained legitimacy in the American academy, this article suggests that critique of the longstanding dichotomy of mind and body necessitates a conciliatory model. I advocate a theory of "embodied cognition" that explains how the human body, despite its condition as an object of culture, exerts subjective influence on the mind. To illustrate how cognition is embodied, I report on an ethnographic study that documented the athletic learning of members of a single women's intercollegiate basketball team.

Mental rotation performance in male soccer players
Jansen, P., Lehmann, J., & Van, D. J. (January 01, 2012). Mental rotation performance in male soccer players. *Plos One, 7*, 10.

It is the main goal of this study to investigate the visual-spatial cognition in male soccer players. Forty males (20 soccer players and 20 non-athletes) solved a chronometric mental rotation task with both cubed and embodied figures (human figures, body postures). The results confirm previous results that all participants had a lower mental rotation speed for cube figures compared to embodied figures and a higher error rate for cube figures, but only at angular disparities greater than 90°. It is a new finding that soccer-players showed a faster reaction time for embodied stimuli. Because rotation speed did not differ between soccer-players and non-athletes this finding cannot be attributed to the mental rotation process itself but instead to differences in one of the following processes which are involved in a mental rotation task: the encoding process, the maintanence of readiness, or the motor process. The results are discussed against the background of the influence on longterm physical activity on mental rotation and the context of embodied cognition.

ATHLETES, SITUATED COGNITION
Elite athletes' differentiated action in trampolining: a qualitative and situated analysis of different levels of performance using retrospective interviews
Hauw, D., & Durand, M. (January 01, 2004). Elite athletes' differentiated action

in trampolining: a qualitative and situated analysis of different levels of performance using retrospective interviews. *Perceptual and Motor Skills, 98,* 3, 1139-52.

Using a situated cognition approach, this study analyzed elite athletes' actions, i.e., behaviors link to cognitions, during competitive trampoline performances, which are evaluated from a succession of 10 acrobatic movements characterized by flight time and fall risk. 27 exercises performed by 10 elite athletes were ranked poor, average, or good and analyzed. Self-confrontation interviews were conducted and transcribed in relation with behavioral descriptions derived from video recordings. Qualitative analysis was performed to identify units of meaningful action and their components. The succession of units describing the stream of actions was used to identify differentiated organization of trampolinists' performances. Three patterns, corresponding to performance levels, were distinguished by (a) an increasing number of meaningful actions occurring at the same time, (b) a reduction in actions of waiting, and (c) the emergence of new actions aimed at interaction with the situation. These results suggest that differentiation in performance level is linked with meaningful actions modified through interaction with the context.

Situated analysis of elite trampolinists' problems in competition using retrospective interviews

Hauw, D., & Durand, M. (January 01, 2007). Situated analysis of elite trampolinists' problems in competition using retrospective interviews. *Journal of Sports Sciences, 25,*2, 173-183.

The aims of this study were to identify and analyse elite athletes' problems in competition. A situated cognition approach placed the emphasis on athletes' actions (i.e. cognitions and behaviours), which were considered to emerge from couplings with selected elements of the context. Fifty-two exercises performed by 10 elite trampolinists were analysed. Field observations, structured interviews, and self-confrontation interviews were conducted and transcribed, and used together with behavioural descriptions derived from video recordings. Performance problems were selected from these reports and from the major infringements of trampoline rules. Qualitative analysis identified the meaningful units of action and their semiotic components for each problem. Four categories of problem were identified and noted to appear either separately or jointly while performing: (a) finding the best moment to begin the performance; (b) finding and maintaining the best mode of involvement to end the performance; (c) recovering normal sensory-motor capacity to perform; and (d) solving problems quickly and definitively while performing. The results suggest that the study of action - situation couplings in sports, as well as of their constantly evolving dynamics, not only reveals elite athletes' psychological activity, but is vital to a deeper understanding of these couplings.

Analysis of elite swimmers' activity during an instrumented protocol

David, A., Poizat, G., Gal-Petitfaux, N., Toussaint, H., & Seifert, M. L. (January 01, 2009). Analysis of elite swimmers' activity during an instrumented protocol. *Journal of Sports Sciences, 27,* 10, 1043-1050.

The aim of this study was to examine swimmers' activity-technical device coupling during an experimental protocol (MAD-system). The study was conducted within a course-of-action theoretical and methodological framework. Two types of data were collected: (a) video recordings and (b) verbalizations during post-protocol interviews. The data were processed in two steps: (a) reconstruction of each swimmer's course of action and (b) comparison of the courses of action. Analysis from the actors' point of view allowed a description of swimmer-technical device coupling. The results showed that the technical device modified the athletes' range of perceptions and repertoire of actions. They also indicated that changes in coupling between the swimmers and the MAD-system were linked to utilization constraints: the swimmers' experiences were transformed in the same speed intervals, suggesting that this was an essential situational constraint to swimmer-technical device coupling. This study highlights how a technical device and the conditions of its use changed athletes' activity and suggests that it is important to develop activity-centred design in sport.

ATHLETES, COGNITIVE ERGONOMICS
The Taskload-Efficiency-Safety-Buffer Triangle - Development and validation with air traffic management
Kallus, K. W., Hoffmann, P., Winkler, H., & Vormayr, E. (January 01, 2010). The Taskload-Efficiency-Safety-Buffer Triangle - Development and validation with air traffic management. *Ergonomics, 53,* 2, 240-246.

The Taskload-Efficiency-Safety-Buffer Triangle (TEST) was developed as a new computerised scaling tool for quickly visualising changes in and trade-offs between the three critical factors that determine the work situation of air traffic management (ATM), i.e. taskload, efficiency and safety-buffers. Based on a task analysis of ATM and backed up by the stress-strain model, an easy-to-interpret triangle was constructed and validated both in simulated and real ATM workplaces. Results from the validation studies show that TEST does not only reflect the most relevant task characteristics, but also provides additional insights in the controllers' working styles. The TEST tool can make ATM safety surveys more efficient and help supervisors to decide about optimal times for opening or closing additional sectors. Statement of Relevance: TEST is a new tool to assess taskload, efficiency and safety-buffers in a joint scaling. It reflects increases in taskload and effects of taskload on safety-buffers and efficiency, as well as trade-offs in opposite directions. This tool might be very useful to check sector capacity in ATM and other high risk environments.

Description of dynamic shared knowledge: an exploratory study during a competitive team sports interaction
Bourbousson, J., Poizat, G., Saury, J., & Seve, C. (January 01, 2011). Description of dynamic shared knowledge: an exploratory study during a competitive team sports interaction. *Ergonomics, 54,* 2, 120-138.

This exploratory case study describes the sharedness of knowledge within a basketball team (nine players) and how it changes during an official match. To determine how knowledge is mobilised in an actual game situation, the data were collected and processed following course-of-action theory (Theureau 2003). The results were used to characterise the contents of the shared knowledge (i.e. regarding teammate characteristics, team functioning, opponent characteristics, opposing team functioning and game conditions) and to identify the characteristic types of change: (a) the reinforcement of a previous element of shared knowledge; (b) the invalidation of an element of shared knowledge; (c) fragmentation of an element of shared knowledge; (d) the creation of a new element of shared knowledge. The discussion deals with the diverse types of change in shared knowledge and the heterogeneous and dynamic nature of common ground within the team. Statement of Relevance:The present case study focused on how the cognitions of individual members of a team coordinate to produce a team performance (e.g. surgical teams in hospitals, military teams) and how the shared knowledge changes during team activity. Traditional methods to increase knowledge sharedness can be enhanced by making use of 'opportunities for coordination' to optimise team adaptiveness.

ATHLETES, SEMIOTICS
Can't Be Standing Up Out There: Communicative Performances of (Dis)Ability in Wheelchair Rugby
Lindemann, K. (January 01, 2008). Can't Be Standing Up Out There: Communicative Performances of (Dis)Ability in Wheelchair Rugby. Text and Performance Quarterly, 28, 98-115.

Sport and performance theory have several important yet underdeveloped intersections. Locating these intersections in the properties of play, both areas are particularly useful in examining displays of the disabled body. Wheelchair rugby is one of the fastest growing and most visible wheelchair sports in the world. Participation in the sport offers many benefits for physically disabled persons. However, these benefits may be undercut by the sport's classification system, which determines who will compete and at what level. This paper highlights tactical performances of disability that challenge ableist assumptions. In these performances, athletes engage in sandbagging, performing more disability to receive a favorable classification from physical therapists. While these fluid, malleable performances of play resist the medicalized gaze that Others disabled persons by affixing disability as a static marker of identity, these performances also ironically foster a form of surveillance that imitates the ableist gaze and reifies traditional notions of ability.

ATHLETES, OBSTACLES
Endurance training adherence in elite junior netball athletes: A test of the theory of planned behaviour and a revised theory of planned behavior
Palmer, C., Burwitz, L., Dyer, A., & Spray, C. (January 01, 2005). Endurance training adherence in elite junior netball athletes: A test of the theory of planned behaviour and a revised theory of planned behaviour. *Journal of Sports Sciences, 23*, 3, 277-288.

This study examined the utility of Ajzen's (1985) theory of planned behaviour and Maddux's (1993) revised theory of planned behaviour to predict endurance training intentions and adherence of elite junior netball athletes. One hundred and fifteen athletes from the England Netball World Class Start Programme were assessed on constructs central to the predictions of the two theories. Adherence to a recommended endurance training programme was recorded in self-report diaries across a 9-week period. Validity for the diaries was supported by significant correlations (P ?<?0.001) with recalls across 7 days and 9 weeks. Adherence was moderate and variable between athletes (mean??=??66.05,

s??=??25.75%). Two separate path analyses were conducted to examine the predictions of the theories. Goodness-of-fit indices suggested acceptable fit of the data to the models. Analyses showed that attitude towards the new behaviour, subjective norms and perceived behavioural control predicted training intentions. The relationship between intention and adherence was weak. The present results suggest that the constructs of the theory of planned behaviour offer some insight into the explanation of intentions to follow an endurance training programme. Constructs unique to the revised theory of planned behaviour did not significantly predict training intentions or behaviour. Implications for practitioners working with team sport performers are provided.

The Functional Theory of Counterfactual Thinking
Epstude, K., & Roese, N. (January 01, 2008). The Functional Theory of Counterfactual Thinking. *Personality and Social Psychology Review, 12*, 2, 168-192.

Counterfactuals are thoughts about alternatives to past events, that is, thoughts of what might have been. This article provides an updated account of the functional theory of counterfactual thinking, suggesting that such thoughts are best explained in terms of their role in behavior regulation and performance improvement. The article reviews a wide range of cognitive experiments indicating that counterfactual thoughts may influence behavior by either of two routes: a content-specific pathway (which involves specific informational effects on behavioral intentions, which then influence behavior) and a content-neutral pathway (which involves indirect effects via affect, mind-sets, or motivation). The functional theory is particularly useful in organizing recent findings regarding counterfactual thinking and mental health. The article concludes by considering the connections to other theoretical conceptions, especially recent advances in goal cognition.

Exercising your brain: A review of human brain plasticity and training-induced learning
Green, C. S., & Bavelier, D. (December 01, 2008). Exercising your brain: A review of human brain plasticity and training-induced learning. *Psychology and Aging, 23*, 4, 692-701.

Human beings have an amazing capacity to learn new skills and adapt to new environments. However, several obstacles remain to be overcome in designing paradigms to broadly improve quality of life. Arguably, the most notable impediment to this goal is that learning tends to be quite specific to the trained regimen and does not transfer to even qualitatively similar tasks. This severely limits the potential benefits of learning to daily life. This review discusses training regimens that lead to the acquisition of new knowledge and strategies that can be used flexibly across a range of tasks and contexts. Possible characteristics of training regimens are proposed that may be responsible for augmented learning, including the manner in which task difficulty is progressed, the motivational state of the learner, and the type of feedback the training provides. When maximally implemented in rehabilitative paradigms, these characteristics may greatly increase the efficacy of training.

Sport and business coaching: Perspective of a sport psychologist
Gordon, S. (January 01, 2007). Sport and business coaching: Perspective of a

sport psychologist. *Australian Psychologist, 42*, 4, 271-282.

This personal perspective on both sport and business coaching psychology practice discusses theories and models utilised by practitioners in both settings. Performance demands and examples of intervention research common to sport and business settings are described, and suggestions on collaborative research projects are offered. Advice that sport leaders have offered business leaders is summarised and a case study example of transformational leadership in sport is provided. In the author's opinion the evidence suggests that coaching psychologists in both performance environments would benefit considerably from more closely linked approaches to applied research.

ATHLETES, MENTAL IMAGERY
Individual differences in mental imagery experience: developmental changes and specialization

Isaac, A. R., & Marks, D. F. (January 01, 1994). Individual differences in mental imagery experience: developmental changes and specialization. *British Journal of Psychology (London, England : 1953), 85*, 479-500.

This research has two purposes: (1) to study developmental changes and differences in visual and movement imagery in male and female children and adults; (2) to investigate whether systematic differences in imagery vividness can be measured in specialist groups. In Study 1, the Vividness of Visual Imagery Questionnaire and the Vividness of Movement Imagery Questionnaire were administered to 547 individuals in age groups from 7-8 to 50+ years of age. Significant increases in imagery vividness were found in females at 8-9 and in males at 10-11 years. In general females report more vivid imagery than males but at about 50 females' movement imagery reduced in vividness. In Studies 2-5 imagery differences in specialist groups were examined using the same two questionnaires with a total of 655 participants. In Study 2, children aged 7-15 years with poor movement control were found to be extremely poor imagers with 42 per cent reporting no imagery at all. In Study 3, physical education students reported more vivid imagery than students specializing in physics, English, and surveying. In Study 4, significant differences were found between elite athletes' imagery and that of matched controls. In Study 5, air traffic controllers and pilots were found to have significantly more vivid imagery than matched control groups. Introspective reports of imagery experience show a systematic pattern of relationships with age, gender, and specialization requiring high-level performance of perceptual motor skills. These findings support the theory that mental imagery plays a key role in the planning and implementation of action.

Effect of mental imagery on the development of skilled motor actions

Fontani, G., Migliorini, S., Benocci, R., Facchini, A., Casini, M., & Corradeschi, F. (January 01, 2007). Effect of mental imagery on the development of skilled motor actions. *Perceptual and Motor Skills, 105*, 3, 803-26.

To test the effect of imagery in the training of skilled movements, an experiment was designed in which athletes learned a new motor action and trained themselves for a month either by overt action or by mental imagery of the action. The experiment was carried out with 30 male karateka (M age = 35 yr., SD = 8.7;

M years of practice = 6, SD = 3) instructed to perform an action (Ura-Shuto-Uchi) that they had not previously learned. The athletes were divided into three groups: Untrained (10 subjects who did not perform any training), Action Trained (10 subjects who performed Ura-Shuto-Uchi training daily for 16 minutes), and Mental Imagery (10 subjects who performed mental imagery training of Ura-Shuto-Uchi daily for 16 minutes). The subjects were tested five times, once every 7 days. During each test, they performed a series of 60 motor action trials. In Tests 1, 3, and 5, they also performed a series of 60 mental imagery trials. During the trials, an electroencephalogram (EEG), electromyography (EMG), muscle strength and power, and other physiological parameters were recorded. The results differed by group. Untrained subjects did not show significant effects. In the Action Trained group, training had an effect on reactivity and movement speed, with a reduction of EMG activation and reaction times. Moreover, muscle strength, power, and work increased significantly. The Mental Imagery group showed the same effects on muscle strength, power, and work, but changes in reactivity were not observed. In the Mental Imagery group, the study of Movement Related Brain Macropotentials indicated a progressive modification of the profile of the waves from Test 1 to Test 5 during imagery, showing significant variations of the amplitude of the waves related to the premotor and motor execution periods. Results show that motor imagery can influence muscular abilities such as strength and power and can modify Movement Related Brain Macropotentials, the profile of which potentially could be used to verify the effectiveness of motor imagery training.

Clinical skills: Learning basic surgical skills with mental imagery: using the simulation centre in the mind
Sanders, C. W., Sadoski, M., van, W. K., Bramson, R., Wiprud, R., & Fossum, T. W. (June 01, 2008). Clinical skills: Learning basic surgical skills with mental imagery: using the simulation centre in the mind. *Medical Education, 42,* 6, 607-612.

Although surgeons and athletes frequently use mental imagery in preparing to perform, mental imagery has not been extensively researched as a learning technique in medical education. A mental imagery rehearsal technique was experimentally compared with textbook study to determine the effects of each on the learning of basic surgical skills. Sixty-four Year 2 medical students were randomly assigned to 2 treatment groups in which they undertook either mental imagery or textbook study. Both groups received the usual skills course of didactic lectures, demonstrations, physical practice with pigs' feet and a live animal laboratory. One group received additional training in mental imagery and the other group was given textbook study. Performance was assessed at 3 different time-points using a reliable rating scale. Analysis of variance on student performance in live rabbit surgery revealed a significant interaction favouring the imagery group over the textbook study group. The mental imagery technique appeared to transfer learning from practice to actual surgery better than textbook study.

Deliberate imagery practice: the development of imagery skills in competitive athletes
Cumming, J., & Hall, C. (February 01, 2002). Deliberate imagery practice: the development of imagery skills in competitive athletes. *Journal of Sports*

Sciences, 20, 2, 137-145.

The aim of this study was to examine mental imagery within the context of the deliberate practice framework. Altogether, 159 athletes from one of three different competitive standards (recreational, provincial and national) completed the Deliberate Imagery Practice Questionnaire, which was designed for the present study to assess the athletes' perceptions of the importance of imagery along the three deliberate practice dimensions of relevancy, concentration and enjoyment. The results indicated that national athletes perceived imagery to be more relevant to performing than recreational athletes. In addition, athletes of a higher standard (i.e. provincial and national) reported using more imagery in a recent typical week and they had accumulated significantly more hours of imagery practice across their athletic career than recreational athletes. Finally, the relationships among the dimensions of deliberate practice did not lend conclusive support to either the original conception of deliberate practice or a sports-specific framework of deliberate practice.

Measurement of motivational imagery abilities in sport
Gregg, M., & Hall, C. (January 01, 2006). Measurement of motivational imagery abilities in sport. *Journal of Sports Sciences, 24*, 9, 961-971.

Athletes report using imagery most often to successfully cope with and master challenging situations. This function of imagery is termed "motivational general-mastery" and includes imagining being focused, confident and in control in difficult circumstances. Also, athletes often use imagery to regulate their arousal levels (e.g. relaxing, psyching up) and this function of imagery is termed "motivational-general arousal". While most athletes report employing these two motivational functions of imagery, their ability to do so has not been examined. The aim of the present study was to develop a measure of motivational general sport imagery ability, the Motivational Imagery Ability Measure for Sport (MIAMS). This was accomplished through three phases. Across these phases, evidence was generated showing that the psychometric properties of the instrument are adequate. In addition, the relationship of scores on the MIAMS to demographic variables, including sex, sport type and competitive standard, were examined. It was found that athletes participating at a competitive level scored higher on the MIAMS than athletes participating at a recreational level.

Is controllability of imagery related to canoe-slalom performance?
MacIntyre, T., Moran, A., & Jennings, D. J. (January 01, 2002). Is controllability of imagery related to canoe-slalom performance?. *Perceptual and Motor Skills, 94*, 3, 1245-50.

This study investigated the relationship of controllability of mental imagery with canoe-slalom performance. Controllability of mental imagery was assessed by an objective test of mental rotation, the Mental Rotations Test. This test was administered to both elite (n = 19) and intermediate (n = 12) athletes. Predictive validity of the controllability test was supported by a significant correlation between test scores and race rank-order for the elite canoeing group (rs = 0.42, p<.05); however, it did not distinguish elite from intermediate groups (t29 = 0.98, p>.05). Researchers should attempt to evaluate vividness of imagery, controllability of imagery, and accuracy of reference to understand more fully the nature of athletes' imagery.

Seeing Future Success: Does Imagery Perspective Influence Achievement Motivation?

Vasquez, N., & Buehler, R. (January 01, 2007). Seeing Future Success: Does Imagery Perspective Influence Achievement Motivation?. *Personality and Social Psychology Bulletin, 33,* 10, 1392-1405.

Imagining future success can sometimes enhance people's motivation to achieve it. This article examines a phenomenological aspect of positive mental imagery— the visual perspective adopted—that may moderate its motivational impact. The authors hypothesize that people feel more motivated to succeed on a future task when they visualize its successful completion from a third-person rather than a first-person perspective. Actions viewed from the third-person perspective are generally construed at a relatively high level of abstraction—in a manner that highlights their larger meaning and significance—which should heighten their motivational impact. Three studies in the domain of academic motivation support this reasoning. Students experience a greater increase in achievement motivation when they imagine their successful task completion from a third- rather than a first-person perspective. Moreover, mediational analyses reveal that third-person imagery boosts motivation by prompting students to construe their success abstractly and to perceive it as important.

Experimental Studies of Psychological Interventions With Athletes in Competitions

Martin, G., Vause, T., & Schwartzman, L. (January 01, 2005). Experimental Studies of Psychological Interventions With Athletes in Competitions. *Behavior Modification, 29,* 4, 616-641.

During the past three decades, behavioral practitioners have been applying techniques to improve the performance of athletes. To what extent are interventions, designed to improve the directly and reliably measured performance of athletes in competitions, based on experimental demonstrations of efficacy? That is the question addressed by this review. All issues of three behavioral journals and seven sport psychology journals, from 1972 through 2002, were examined for articles that addressed the above question. Fifteen articles were found that met the inclusion criteria, yielding an average of only one published study every 2 years. This article reviews those articles, discusses reasons for the dearth of research in this area, and makes recommendations for much needed future research.

Re-imagining motor imagery: building bridges between cognitive neuroscience and sport psychology

Moran, A., Guillot, A., Macintyre, T., & Collet, C. (January 01, 2012). Re-imagining motor imagery: building bridges between cognitive neuroscience and sport psychology. *British Journal of Psychology (london, England : 1953), 103,* 2, 224-47.

One of the most remarkable capacities of the mind is its ability to simulate sensations, actions, and other types of experience. A mental simulation process that has attracted recent attention from cognitive neuroscientists and sport psychologists is motor imagery or the mental rehearsal of actions without engaging in the actual physical movements involved. Research on motor imagery is important in psychology because it provides an empirical window on consciousness and movement planning, rectifies a relative neglect of non-visual types of mental imagery, and has practical implications for skill learning and skilled performance in special populations (e.g., athletes, surgeons). Unfortunately, contemporary research on motor imagery is hampered by a variety of semantic, conceptual, and methodological issues that prevent cross-fertilization of ideas between cognitive neuroscience and sport psychology. In this paper, we review these issues, suggest how they can be resolved, and sketch some potentially fruitful new directions for inter-disciplinary research in motor imagery.

Relation between sport and spatial imagery: comparison of three groups of participants

Ozel, S., Larue, J., & Molinaro, C. (January 01, 2004). Relation between sport and spatial imagery: comparison of three groups of participants. *The Journal of Psychology, 138*, 1, 49-63.

The literature suggests that sport may be considered a spatial activity and that engaging in spatial activities increases the capacity of an individual to implement mental imagery. Moreover, mental rotation calls upon motor processes that are heavily involved in sporting activities. For these reasons, the authors hypothesized that athletes ought to perform mental rotation tasks better than nonathletes. Also, athletes trained to react quickly to constantly changing environments should be faster at processing the information in a mental rotation task than athletes operating in more settled environments. The results of this study show that athletes performed the mental rotation task significantly faster than nonathletes. These results support the suggestion that there is a link between sport and the ability to perform mental image transformations; however, this ability may not be specific to the conditions in which the athlete performs.

Pre-competitive confidence, coping, and subjective performance in sport

Levy, A. R., Nicholls, A. R., & Polman, R. C. (January 01, 2011). Pre-competitive confidence, coping, and subjective performance in sport. *Scandinavian Journal of Medicine & Science in Sports, 21*, 5, 721-9.

The primary aim of this study was to investigate the relationship between confidence and subjective performance in addition to exploring whether coping mediated this relationship. A sample of 414 athletes completed a measure of confidence before performance. Athletes also completed a measure of coping and subjective performance after competing. Correlational findings revealed that confidence was positively and significantly associated with subjective performance. Furthermore, mediational analysis found that coping partly mediated this relationship. In particular, task-oriented coping (i.e., mental imagery) and disengagement-oriented coping (i.e., resignation) had positive and negative mediational effects, respectively. Additionally, athletes who employed mental imagery generally coped more effectively than those using resignation. These findings imply mental imagery has the potential not only to improve confidence, but also subsequent performance, while resignation coping may have the opposite effect. Overall, these results lend some credence to Vealey's integrated sports confidence model.

Self-Talk and Sports Performance: A Meta-Analysis
Hatzigeorgiadis, A., Zourbanos, N., Galanis, E., & Theodorakis, Y. (January 01, 2011). Self-Talk and Sports Performance: A Meta-Analysis. *Perspectives on Psychological Science, 6,* 4, 348-356.

Based on the premise that what people think influences their actions, self-talk strategies have been developed to direct and facilitate human performance. In this article, we present a meta-analytic review of the effects of self-talk interventions on task performance in sport and possible factors that may moderate the effectiveness of self-talk. A total of 32 studies yielding 62 effect sizes were included in the final meta-analytic pool. The analysis revealed a positive moderate effect size (ES = .48). The moderator analyses showed that self-talk interventions were more effective for tasks involving relatively fine, compared with relatively gross, motor demands, and for novel, compared with well-learned, tasks. Instructional self-talk was more effective for fine tasks than was motivational self-talk; moreover, instructional self-talk was more effective for fine tasks rather than gross tasks. Finally, interventions including self-talk training were more effective than those not including self-talk training. The results of this study establish the effectiveness of self-talk in sport, encourage the use of self-talk as a strategy to facilitate learning and enhance performance, and provide new research directions.

Mental toughness, optimism, pessimism, and coping among athletes
Nicholls, A. R., Polman, R. C. J., Levy, A. R., & Backhouse, S. H. (January 01, 2008). Mental toughness, optimism, pessimism, and coping among athletes. *Personality and Individual Differences, 44,* 5, 1182-1192.

The concept of mental toughness is widely used, but empirical evidence is required to fully understand this construct and its related variables. The purpose of this paper was to explore the relationship between: (a) mental toughness and coping, (b) mental toughness and optimism, and (c) coping and optimism. Participants were 677 athletes (male 454; female 223) aged between 15 and 58 years (M age = 22.66 years, SD = 7.20). Mental toughness correlated significantly with 8 of the 10 coping subscales and optimism. In particular, higher levels of mental toughness were associated with more problem or approach coping strategies (mental imagery, effort expenditure, thought control, and logical analysis) but less use of avoidance coping strategies (distancing, mental distraction, and resignation). Eight coping subscales were significantly correlated with optimism and pessimism. In conclusion, the relationships observed in this study emphasize the need for the inclusion of coping and optimism training in mental toughness interventions.

Where's the Emotion? How Sport Psychology Can Inform Research on Emotion in Human Factors
Eccles, D., Ward, P., Woodman, T., Janelle, C., Le, S. C., Ehrlinger, J., Castanier, C., ... Coombes, S. (January 01, 2011). Where's the Emotion? How Sport Psychology Can Inform Research on Emotion in Human Factors. *Human Factors, 53,* 2, 180-202.

The aim of this study was to demonstrate how research on emotion in sport psychology might inform the field of human factors. Background: Human factors historically has paid little attention to the role of emotion within the research on human-system relations. The theories, methods, and practices related to research on emotion within sport psychology might be informative for human factors because fundamentally, sport psychology and human factors are applied fields concerned with enhancing performance in complex, real-world domains. Method: Reviews of three areas of theory and research on emotion in sport psychology are presented, and the relevancy of each area for human factors is proposed: (a) emotional preparation and regulation for performance, (b) an emotional trait explanation for risk taking in sport, and (c) the link between emotion and motor behavior. Finally, there are suggestions for how to continue cross-talk between human factors and sport psychology about research on emotion and related topics in the future. Results: The relevance of theory and research on emotion in sport psychology for human factors is demonstrated. Conclusion: The human factors field and, in particular, research on human-system relations may benefit from a consideration of theory and research on emotion in sport psychology. Application: Theories, methods, and practices from sport psychology might be applied usefully to human factors.

Cognitive behavioural strategies and anxiety in elite orienteers

Gal-Or, Y., Tenenbaum, G., & Shimrony, S. (January 01, 1986). Cognitive behavioural strategies and anxiety in elite orienteers. *Journal of Sports Sciences, 4,* 1, 39-48.

The primary purpose of this exploratory field study was to examine the use of cognitive behavioural strategies by highly skilled orienteers prior to and during competition. A secondary purpose of the study was to investigate whether differences in the level of qualification in orienteering is related to state anxiety. The subjects were divided into three classes with respect to their international and national records. The first two classes (A and B) were composed of international and national level athletes. The third class (C) included orienteers with unknown international records. Examination of the use of behavioural cognitive strategies during competition indicated that all orienteers reported a moderate use of mental imagery, above moderate use of inner talk and a focus of attention on present action rather than past or future. The other major findings were that prior to competition, superior orienteers reported use of higher self-efficacy, more positive outcome expectations and more task demand orientation than their less successful counterparts. Top orienteers coped more successfully with pre competition anxiety by lowering their anxiety to a more moderate level prior to the actual performance.

Emotions and Golf Performance

Cohen, A., Tenenbaum, G., & English, R. (January 01, 2006). Emotions and Golf Performance. *Behavior Modification, 30,* 3, 259-280.

A multiple case study investigation is reported in which emotions and performance were assessed within the probabilistic individual zone of optimal functioning (IZOF) model (Kamata, Tenenbaum,& Hanin, 2002) to develop idiosyncratic emotion-performance profiles. These profiles were incorporated into a psychological skills training (PST) intervention, with a focus on three emotional dimensions, that is, arousal, pleasantness, and functionality, and several psychological strategies employed during practice and competition. Two female varsity golfers at a major Division I university in the Southeast participated in the case study during the Spring 2002 season. The PST intervention resulted in enhanced emotional self-regulation skills and improved golf performance. Directions for future research into the IZOF model and implications for practical application of the model are discussed.

Psychological Hallmarks of Skilled Golfers
Hellstrom, J. (January 01, 2009). Psychological Hallmarks of Skilled Golfers. *Sports Medicine, 39,* 10, 845-855.

In this article, the psychological hallmarks of skilled golfers (professionals and amateurs with handicaps of le4) are investigated. Professional golfers believe that attitude, desire and motivation are important psychological qualities necessary to succeed in tournaments. They are committed to golf, have goals they strive for, make plans, evaluate their performance and systematically train towards improving their game. The study of skilled golfers' traits, as measured by 16 personality factors, has provided ambiguous results and there may be more complex associations not yet investigated in golf. The effect of mood and emotions on golf scores seems to be individual. Differences in personality may explain why mood states, measured by mood state profiles, have not shown a strong correlation to golf scores. Task focus, confidence, imagery, patience, ability to focus on one shot at a time and performing automatically have been found to be important during competition. These variables need to be further researched before, during and after the swing. The psychological processes needed before, during and after the swing differ and should be further specified. A decrease in heart rate and a lower cortical activity moment before the swing may be signs of an optimal performance state. The effect of coping strategies may vary over time, and players should be able to switch and combine different strategies. Pre-shot routine is associated with performance. However, it is not clear if consistency of total duration and behavioural content in pre-shot routine cause improved performance. Pre-shot routine may also be an effect of psychological processes, such as a different task focus. It may facilitate an automatic execution of technique, which can lead to better performance. The psychological variables needed for competitive golf should be related to the physical, technical and game-statistical variables in coaching and future research.

Mood responses to athletic performance in extreme environments
Lane, A., Terry, P., Stevens, M., Barney, S., & Dinsdale, S. (January 01, 2004). Mood responses to athletic performance in extreme environments. *Journal of Sports Sciences, 22,* 10, 886-897.

Competition at elite level can require athletes to perform optimally in extreme environmental conditions. This review focuses on mood responses in such conditions and proposes practical guidelines for those working with athletes. Different environments are considered, including altitude and extreme heat and cold. Performing in extreme heat, cold or at altitude can produce a stress response characterized by increased negative mood and relatively poor performance. Positive adaptations to extreme conditions can be accelerated, but the rate of adaptation appears to be highly individualized. Monitoring mood responses to training under normal conditions provides a basis for identifying the psychological effects of extreme conditions. It is suggested that practitioners carefully monitor the interplay between vigour, fatigue and depressed mood. Reductions in vigour and increases in fatigue are normal responses to hard training, but other aspects of mood disturbance, especially symptoms of depressed mood - however small - may be indicative of a maladaptive response, and practitioners should consider intervening when such symptoms first appear.

Does mental practice enhance performance?
Driskell, J. E., Copper, C., & Moran, A. (August 01, 1994). Does mental practice enhance performance?. *Journal of Applied Psychology, 79,* 4, 481-492.

Mental practice is the cognitive rehearsal of a task prior to performance. Although most researchers contend that mental practice is an effective means of enhancing performance, a clear consensus is precluded because (1) mental practice is often defined so loosely as to include almost any type of mental preparation and (2) empirical results are inconclusive. A meta-analysis of the literature on mental practice was conducted to determine the effect of mental practice on performance and to identify conditions under which mental practice is most effective. Results indicate that mental practice has a positive and significant effect on performance, and the effectiveness of mental practice is moderated by the type of task, the retention interval between practice and performance, and the length or duration of the mental practice intervention.

Measuring motor imagery ability: A review
McAvinue, L., & Robertson, I. (January 01, 2008). Measuring motor imagery ability: A review. *European Journal of Cognitive Psychology, 20,* 2, 232-251.

The internal nature of motor imagery makes the measurement of motor imagery ability a difficult task. In this review, we describe and evaluate existing measures of motor imagery ability. Following Jeannerod (1994, 1997) we define motor imagery in terms of imagined movement from the first person perspective. We describe how explicit motor imagery ability can be measured by questionnaire and mental chronometry, and how implicit motor imagery ability can be measured through prospective action judgement and motorically driven perceptual decision paradigms. Future research should be directed towards a theoretical analysis of motor imagery ability, the improvement of existing questionnaires and the development of new ones, and the standardisation of existing paradigms.

Motor Imagery May Incorporate Trial-to-Trial Error
Valdez, A., & Amazeen, E. (January 01, 2010). Motor Imagery May Incorporate Trial-to-Trial Error. *Journal of Motor Behavior, 42,* 4, 241-256.

The authors tested for 1/f noise in motor imagery (MI). Participants pointed and imagined pointing to a single target (Experiment 1), to targets of varied size (Experiment 2), and switched between pointing and grasping (Experiment 3). Experiment 1 showed comparable patterns of serial correlation in actual and imagined movement. Experiment 2 suggested increased correlation for MI and performance with increased task difficulty, perhaps reflecting adaptation to a more complex environment. Experiment 3 suggested a parallel decrease in correlation with task switching, perhaps reflecting discontinuity of mental set. Although present results do not conclusively reveal 1/f fluctuation, the emergent patterns suggest that MI could incorporate trial-to-trial error across a range of constraints.

Competition stress in sport performers: Stressors experienced in the competition environment

Mellalieu, S., Neil, R., Hanton, S., & Fletcher, D. (January 01, 2009). Competition stress in sport performers: Stressors experienced in the competition environment. *Journal of Sports Sciences, 27*, 7, 729-744.

We examined the performance and organizational stressors encountered by elite and non-elite athletes within the competition environment. Twelve sport performers (6 elite, 6 non-elite) were interviewed about both performance and organizational-related demands experienced when preparing for competition. The framework presented identifies five performance (i.e. preparation, injury, expectations, self-presentation, and rivalry) and five organizational (i.e. factors intrinsic to the sport, roles in the sport organization, sport relationships and interpersonal demands, athletic career and performance development issues, and organizational structure and climate of the sport) stress sources. A similar quantity of performance (#PS) and organizational (#OS) stressors were encountered by elite performers (#PS=127; #OS=72) as by non-elite athletes (#PS=123; #OS=74), with some demands being common and others unique to each group. Although the findings suggest that, prior to competing, sport performers encounter more stressors pertinent to performance than those emanating from the organization, these observations highlight that all the demands faced by athletes should be considered when preparing and implementing interventions to manage competition stress.

Performance and human factors: considerations about cognition and attention for self-paced and externally-paced events

Singer, R. (January 01, 2000). Performance and human factors: considerations about cognition and attention for self-paced and externally-paced events. *Ergonomics, 43*, 10, 1661-1680.

The cognitive psychology school of thought has spawned models of sequential stages or phases of information processing associated with various tasks. It has encouraged the study of cognitions and attention as related to learning, performance and high levels of achievement in goal-directed complex activities in which movement is the medium of expression. Although more recently proposed dynamical systems models challenge the simplicity of this approach, there is little doubt that the ability to learn as well as to excel in performing movement skills depends to a great degree on the effective self-regulation of cognitive processes in a variety of situations. What to think about (or not think about) prior to, during and even after an event can have great consequences on present and subsequent performance. Relevant externally-provided and selfgenerated strategies should enable these processes to function at an optimal level, and are the subject of an increasing amount of research. For such purposes, it is convenient to categorize events as self-paced (closed) and externally-paced (open). Examples of both types of events exist in sport as well as in various occupations and recreational activities, with different information processing demands associated with each one. Any breakdown in a particular stage of processing will potentially lead to poorer performance. Special training techniques and strategies are evolving from the cognitive and psychophysiological research literature that might improve the level of functioning at each stage for either self-paced or externally-paced skills.

Emotions, coping strategies, and performance: A conceptual framework for defining affect-related performance zones

Tenenbaum, G., Edmonds, W. A., & Eccles, D. W. (January 01, 2008). Emotions, coping strategies, and performance: A conceptual framework for defining affect-related performance zones. *Military Psychology, 20.*

This article presents the crisis theory (Bar Eli & Tenenbaum, 1989) and its related approach for determining individual affect-related performance zones (IAPZ: Kamata, Tenenbaum, & Hanin, 2002). The theory and methodology delineate the uniqueness of each individual's ability to appraise stressful conditions and perceive them as functional or dysfunctional to his performance. In addition, the theory and methodology allow incorporating self-regulatory behaviors and coping strategies used during the encounter with situations, which vary in stress appraisal. The article also describes coping mechanisms used to energize (i.e., activate) and relax persons facing situations that vary in cognitive, physical, and affective demands. In particular, the use of imagery and self-talk as coping strategies in stressful situations are presented in more details. Since performance of military personnel involves substantially stressful circumstances (Wallenius, Larsson, & Johansson, 2004), the article advises how sport psychology theories, methodology, and findings can be used in the military environment.

Cognitive-behavioral strategies and precompetitive anxiety among recreational athletes

Ryska, T. A. (December 07, 1998). Cognitive-behavioral strategies and precompetitive anxiety among recreational athletes. *The Psychological Record, 48,* 4, 697-708.

Although cognitive-behavioral strategies have been demonstrated relatively effective in improving sport performance and regulating various affective states among highly skilled athletes, the strategy-anxiety relationship has been left largely untested within the realm of recreational sport. The present study utilized self-report data from 186 recreational league tennis players in order to describe the prevalence, types, sources, and perceived effectiveness of cognitive-behavioral strategy use among a sub-elite sample as well as to determine the extent to which each strategy contributed to changes in cognitive anxiety, somatic anxiety, and self-confidence prior to official competition. Nearly 30[percent] of the sample reported using strategies in training and competition, comprised by relaxation, mental imagery, attention control, positive self-talk, and goal-setting. Stepwise regression analyses controlling for player characteristics revealed that attentional control and goal-setting strategies contributed to lower cognitive state anxiety, attention control and imagery/relaxation strategies resulted in lower somatic state anxiety, and attention control and positive self-talk contributed to increased state self-confidence. The role of specific cognitive-behavioral techniques in facilitating adaptability to competitive stress among recreational athletes is discussed.

Investigating the theoretical significance of research on expertise, mental imagery, and attention in athletes

Darini, M. (March 01, 2011). Investigating the theoretical significance of research on expertise, mental imagery, and attention in athletes. *International Journal of Academic Research, 3*, 2.)

There has been a new upsurge of research enthusiasm in the scientific study of mental processes (e.g., mental imagery) in athletes or the cognitive sport psychology. In spite of this interest, a prominent query has been neglected. Particularly, is research on cognitive procedures in athletes' influential outside sport psychology, in the \"parent\" field of cognitive psychology or in the novel discipline of cognitive neuroscience? The objective of this manuscript is to investigate the theoretical significance of research on expertise, mental imagery and attention in athletes from the aspect of cognitive neuroscience and cognitive psychology. Following analyses of recent paradigm shifts in cognitive neuroscience and cognitive psychology, a narrative survey is provided of main studies on expertise, mental imagery and attention in athletes. This manuscript shows that cognitive psychology in sport has contributed significantly to theoretical comprehending of special mental procedures studied in cognitive neuroscience and cognitive psychology. It also reveals that neuro-scientific investigation on motor imagery cold benefit from increased collaboration with cognitive psychology in sport. Overall, it is concluded that the field of sport offers cognitive investigators a dynamic and rich natural laboratory in which to survey how the mind works.

An interpretative phenomenological analysis of how professional dance teachers implement psychological skills training in practice

Klockare, E., Gustafsson, H., & Nordin-Bates, S. (January 01, 2011). An interpretative phenomenological analysis of how professional dance teachers implement psychological skills training in practice. *Research in Dance Education, 12*, 3, 277-293.

The aim of this study was to examine how dance teachers work with psychological skills with their students in class. Semi-structured interviews were conducted with six female professional teachers in jazz, ballet and contemporary dance. The interview transcripts were analyzed using interpretative phenomenological analysis (Smith 1996). Results revealed that all teachers used psychological skills training techniques such as goal setting and imagery and worked toward the following outcomes: group cohesion, self-confidence, and anxiety management. They strove to create a task-involving climate in their classes and the students were encouraged to participate in, for instance, the goal setting process and imagery applications. The teachers also placed significant emphasis on performance preparation, evaluation, and feedback, although some found it difficult to give positive feedback. Many of the findings can be associated with contemporary theories in sport psychology. However, the dance teachers had almost no formal training in performance psychology, but had instead developed their teaching methodology through their own experiences. Further skills development and suggestions for future research are discussed.

Talent identification and development in dance: a review of the literature
Walker, I., Nordin-Bates, S., & Redding, E. (January 01, 2010). Talent identification and development in dance: a review of the literature. *Research in Dance Education, 11*, 3, 167-191.

Talent identification and development processes are important components of many dance programmes, yet talent is notoriously difficult to define and its identification may rely on intuitive judgements. Taking a systematic approach to the study of dance talent could enable researchers and educators to better determine what talent actually is, the multi-faceted components that exist within talent and subsequently how best it can be optimised. The aim of this paper is to review existing literature relating to aspects of dance talent. While not attempting to define talent nor provide a guide for identification, the review reports on existing relevant literature that describes the characteristics associated with talent in the hope that it will be valuable to educators and researchers. Further research into the characteristics of talented dancers may enable teachers to prepare their students optimally for the exciting opportunities that dance can offer.

ATHLETES, WAYFINDING
Experts' circumvention of processing limitations: An example from the sport of orienteering
Eccles, D. W. (January 01, 2008). Experts' circumvention of processing limitations: An example from the sport of orienteering. *Military Psychology, 20.*

This article provides a discussion of how experts in the sport of orienteering are able to circumvent natural limits on information processing during performance and thus acquire a performance advantage. Orienteering requires navigation in outdoor environments and thus research on skill acquisition in orienteering is of relevance to an understanding of military tasks involving navigation and their training. It is also argued that insight into how experts in general circumvent natural limits on processing is of relevance to an understanding of performance on high-tempo, high-workload tasks common in military settings. Findings from a series of studies of orienteering show how expert orienteers develop various strategies that change the way task-relevant information is mentally processed or displayed in the environment prior to being processed in order to circumvent processing limitations. Implications of this research for training in navigation-based military tasks and other military-related tasks are discussed.

Baseball outfielders maintain a linear optical trajectory when tracking uncatchable fly balls
Shaffer, D. M., & McBeath, M. K. (April 01, 2002). Baseball outfielders maintain a linear optical trajectory when tracking uncatchable fly balls *Journal of Experimental Psychology: Human Perception and Performance, 28*, 2, 335-348.

The authors investigated whether behavior of fielders pursuing uncatchable fly balls supported either (a) maintenance of a linear optical trajectory (LOT) with monotonic increases in optical ball height or (b) maintenance of optical acceleration cancellation (OAC) with simultaneous lateral alignment with the ball. Past work supports usage of both LOT and OAC strategies in the pursuit of catchable balls headed to the side. When balls are uncatchable, fielders must choose either optical linearity or alignment at the expense of the other. Fielders maintained the LOT strategy more often and for a longer period of time than they did the OAC alignment strategy. Findings support the LOT strategy as primary when pursuing balls headed to the side, whether catchable or not.

ATHLETES, BODY ORIENTATION
Maintenance of body orientation in the flight phase of long jumping
Herzog, W. (January 01, 1986). Maintenance of body orientation in the flight phase of long jumping. *Medicine and Science in Sports and Exercise, 18*, 2, 231-41.

The purpose of this investigation was to examine the contributions of the various body segments to the maintenance of body orientation during the flight phase of the long jump. Proper maintenance of body orientation was defined to be achieved if the net angular displacement of the head-and-trunk segment was zero during the flight phase of the long jump. To achieve a zero net angular displacement of the head-and-trunk segment a long jumper needs to execute appropriate arm and leg movements relative to the head-and-trunk segment to counteract the effects of the whole body transverse centroidal angular momentum imparted at takeoff. The contributions of arm and leg movements to the maintenance of body orientation are discussed for the specific cases of a sail and a 2 1/2 hitch-kick long jump. Inherent weaknesses of the sail and hitch-kick techniques, as well as specific weaknesses of two athletes executing these techniques, are discussed with reference to body orientation during the flight phase of the long jump.

How is body orientation controlled during somersaulting?
Bardy, B. G., & Laurent, M. (June 01, 1998). How is body orientation controlled during somersaulting?. *Journal of Experimental Psychology: Human Perception and Performance, 24*, 3, 963-977.

How body orientation is controlled during somersaulting was investigated in 2 experiments that analyzed the kinematics of 223 backward standing somersaults. In Experiment 1, open-loop, initial-condition (flight duration), and prospective (time to contact, or TC_1) control strategies were tested as candidates for the regulation of body moment of inertia during the jump. Decreasing between-trials variability of body orientation over time as well as a negative correlation between body angular velocity and TC_1 suggested that the moment of inertia was regulated prospectively. In Experiment 2, the visual basis for this regulation was examined by asking experts and novices to execute somersaults either with eyes closed or open. Results showed that the prospective regulation observed in the vision condition disappeared in the no-vision condition with the experts, arguing in favor of a visual control during the jump. Such a coupling was absent with the novices, thus illustrating the role played by the perception–action cycle in the learning process.

Trust my face: Cognitive factors of head fakes in sports
Kunde, W., Skirde, S., & Weigelt, M. (June 01, 2011). Trust my face: Cognitive factors of head fakes in sports. *Journal of Experimental Psychology: Applied, 17*, 2, 110-127.

In many competitive sports, players try to deceive their opponents about their behavioral intentions by using specific body movements or postures called fakes. For example, fakes are performed in basketball when a player gazes in one direction but passes or shoots the ball in another direction to avert efficient defense actions. The present study aimed to identify the cognitive processes that underlie the effects of fakes. The paradigmatic situation studied was the head fake in basketball. Observers (basketball novices) had to decide as quickly as possible whether a basketball player would pass a ball to the left or to the right. The player's head and gaze were oriented in the direction of an intended pass or in the opposite direction (i.e., a head fake). Responding was delayed for incongruent compared to congruent directions of the player's gaze and the pass. This head fake effect was independent of response speed, the presence of a fake in the immediately preceding trial, and practice with the task. Five further experiments using additive-factors logic and locus-of-slack logic revealed a perceptual rather than motor-related origin of this effect: Turning the head in a direction opposite the pass direction appears to hamper the perceptual encoding of pass direction, although it does not induce a tendency to move in the direction of the head's orientation. The implications of these results for research on deception in sports and their relevance for sports practice are discussed.

Posturographic testing and motor learning predictability in gymnasts

Carrick, F., Oggero, E., Pagnacco, G., Brock, J. B., & Arikan, T. (January 01, 2007). Posturographic testing and motor learning predictability in gymnasts. *Disability &; Rehabilitation, 29,* 24, 1881-1889.

One aim of this study was to find if there was a difference between balance and stability between elite level gymnasts and non-gymnasts. Another aim was to find if there was a relationship between dynamic posturographic scores associated with sway fatigue or adaptability and the ability to learn new gymnastic routines. The ultimate aim of the study was to improve gymnastic performance while reducing the probability of injury. Methods. Computer dynamic posturography (CDP) provided stability scores, fatigability ratios and adaptation ratios in elite level gymnasts and non-gymnasts controls. Relationships between the postural integrity of gymnasts and non-gymnasts were calculated. The gymnasts were trained in a novel gymnastic routine and performance outcomes were compared to the CDP outcomes. Results. Tests of postural stability have shown that gymnasts have greater postural stability than non-gymnasts. Gymnasts whose adaptability scores were higher were able to learn and perform new motor routines better than those with lower adaptability scores or high fatigability ratios. Conclusions. While gymnasts have greater postural integrity than do non-gymnasts, CDP can identify individuals whose ability to perform new motor activities might be impaired. Methodology to improve functional stability not associated with the motor task may contribute to increased sports performance and decreased probability of injury.

ATHLETES, ENVIRONMENTAL INTERACTION
A review of primary and secondary influences on sport expertise

Baker, J., & Horton, S. (January 01, 2004). A review of primary and secondary influences on sport expertise. *High Ability Studies, 15,* 2, 211-228.

Sport scientists have examined numerous factors influencing the acquisition and manifestation of high levels of performance. These factors can be divided into variables having a primary influence on expertise and variables that have a secondary influence through their interaction with other variables. Primary influences on expertise include genetic, training, and psychological factors while secondary influences include socio-cultural and contextual elements. This paper reviews the factors affecting the development of expert performance in sport and suggests directions for future research.

ATHLETES, PRACTICE
Mental Practice Among Olympic Athletes
Ungerleider, S., & Golding, J. M. (June 01, 1991). Mental Practice Among Olympic Athletes. *Perceptual and Motor Skills, 72,* 3, 1007.

Recent research has focused on the relation of mental rehearsal, specifically visualization, to enhanced performance. Some have suggested that mental practice enhances performance on cognitive tasks more than on motoric ones. The present study describes two waves of survey data from elite track and field athletes before the 1988 US Olympic trials (n=633) and those same athletes after the Olympic Games in Seoul (n=450). The focus was on several measures of mental practice and visualization, including internal and external perspectives and association with sociodemographic data, prior collegiate experience, coaching iduences, and Olympic team selection. Analyses suggest that mental practice may be associated with more successful track and field performance for selected groups of athletes.

"Practice makes perfect:" retest effects in college athletes
Macciocchi, S. N. (January 01, 1990). "Practice makes perfect:" retest effects in college athletes. *Journal of Clinical Psychology, 46,* 5, 628-31.

Retest effects on a diverse set of neuropsychological measures were established using a normal sample comprised of college athletes (N = 110). Results suggest that retest effects vary depending on the type of test used, but the magnitude of effect on individual tests can be quite large. Implications of using tests with large retest effects or tests without established retest effect sizes are discussed.

Influence of practice characteristics on injury risk in young athletes
Frisch, A., Urhausen, A., Seil, R., Windal, T., Agostinis, H., Croisier, J. L., & Theisen, D. (April 01, 2011). Influence of practice characteristics on injury risk in young athletes. *British Journal of Sports Medicine, 45,* 4.

Background Prior research has identified athlete-related risk factors associated with increased sports injury rate. Practice characteristics of young athletes have never been investigated in this respect.
Objective: To assess the injury problem in a multi-sport setting of young athletes and to determine practice-related risk factors.
Design: Prospective epidemiological study.
Setting: Follow-up of young athletes of a Luxembourgish sport school from September 2008 to July 2009 (42 weeks).
Participants: 190 athletes (14.9 ± 1.6 years) (65% boys) from 16 different sport disciplines.
Assessment of risk factors: Practice-related characteristics (context, volume,

frequency and subjective intensity).
Main outcome measurements: Data pertaining to training and competition were recorded daily for each athlete. Standardised injury characteristics were registered. An injury was defined as an incident occurring during sport practice preventing the athlete to participate in at least one full training session or game.
Results: From the 190 athletes, 74% sustained at least one injury during the observation period. Injury rate was 1.65 injuries per athlete; injury incidence was 3.72 injuries/1000 h. The risk of injury was six times higher (CI95% (4.70–8.12)) in competition than in training (13.60 and 1.96 injuries/1000 h, respectively). Two thirds of the injuries were of intrinsic nature (27% progressive and 40% acute non-contact injuries). In team sports athletes having sustained at least one intrinsic injury had, compared to those with no intrinsic injury, a lower number of practice sessions per day (0.83 versus 0.89 sessions/day; p=0.023), a higher percentage of intense sessions (40 versus 30%; p=0.007), a higher number of intense sessions per day (0.33 versus 0.27 sessions/day; p=0.047) and a higher proportion of days with two intense sessions (5.7% versus 2.7%; p=0.007).
Conclusion: The relationship between practice characteristics and sports injuries should be further studied and might point to interesting prevention initiatives, provided that sports practice can be monitored.

"Imagine that!": How coaches advise their athletes to use imagery in practice settings
Kelling, M. R., Short, S. E., & Ross-Stewart, L. (July 02, 2007). "Imagine that!": How coaches advise their athletes to use imagery in practice settings. *Journal of Sport & Exercise Psychology, 29.*

No abstract available

How college basketball coaches advise their athletes to use imagery in practice settings
Olson, J. D., Short, S. E., & Short, M. W. (July 02, 2007). How college basketball coaches advise their athletes to use imagery in practice settings. *Journal of Sport & Exercise Psychology, 29.*

No abstract available

EXPERT RIDERS, PRACTICE
Differences in motor imagery time when predicting task duration in alpine skiers and equestrian riders
Louis, M., Collet, C., Champely, S., & Guillot, A. (January 01, 2012). Differences in motor imagery time when predicting task duration in alpine skiers and equestrian riders. *Research Quarterly for Exercise and Sport, 83,* 1, 86-93.

Athletes' ability to use motor imagery (MI) to predict the speed at which they could perform a motor sequence has received little attention. In this study, 21 alpine skiers and 16 equestrian riders performed MI based on a prediction of actual performance time (a) after the course inspection, (b) before the start, and (c) after the actual performance. MI and physical times were similar in expert skiers during each imagery session, while novice skiers and novice and expert riders underestimated the actual course duration. These findings provide evidence that the temporal accuracy of an imagery task prediction depends on the performer's expertise level and characteristics of the motor skill.

The effects of anxiety and strategic planning on visual search behavior
Moran, A., Byrne, A., & McGlade, N. (March 01, 2002). The effects of anxiety and strategic planning on visual search behaviour. *Journal of Sports Sciences, 20*, 3, 225-236.

The past decade has witnessed increased interest in the visual search behaviour of athletes. Little is known, however, about the relationship between anxiety and eye movements in sport performers or about the extent to which athletes' planned and actual visual search strategies correspond. To address these issues, we conducted two studies. In Study 1, eight expert female gymnasts were presented with three digital slides of a model performing a skill that is known to be anxiety-provoking in this sport - namely, the 'back flip' on the beam. By varying the height of the beam and the presence or absence of safety mats, the slides differed in the amount of anxiety that they elicited vicariously in the viewer. In the study, the gymnasts were asked to imagine themselves in the position of the depicted model and to describe the anxiety that they felt. As they viewed the slides, their eye movements were recorded. As predicted, anxiety was associated with an increase in the number of fixations to peripheral areas. In addition, the more 'threatening' slides elicited significantly more fixations than the less feared images. In Study 2, the plans of 15 equestrian performers (5 expert, 5 intermediate and 5 novice) were elicited as they engaged in a virtual 'walk' around a computerized show-jumping course. Contrary to expectations, the congruence between intended and actual search behaviour was not significantly greater for expert riders than for the less skilled groups. Also, the fact that the top riders allocated more fixations to slides than the less skilled performers challenged the prediction that expertise would be associated with economy of visual search. Finally, as expected, the expert riders were significantly less dependent on the overall 'course plan' than the intermediate and novice equestrian performers when inspecting the fences.

Towards a conceptual model of motorcyclists' Risk Awareness: A comparative study of riding experience effect on hazard detection and situational criticality assessment
Bellet, T., & Banet, A. (November 01, 2012). Towards a conceptual model of motorcyclists' Risk Awareness: A comparative study of riding experience effect on hazard detection and situational criticality assessment. *Accident Analysis and Prevention, 49*, 154-164.

This research investigates risk awareness abilities among different populations of motorcyclists. Risk awareness is defined here as an extension of the Situational Awareness theory applied to critical driving situations. This study is more particularly focused on two main cognitive abilities supporting risk awareness: hazard detection, corresponding to riders' skill to perceive critical event occurring in the road environment and to identify it as a threat, and situational criticality assessment, corresponding to a subjective assessment of the accident risk. From this theoretical framework, the aim is to compare motorcyclists' performances in risk awareness according to their experience in motorcycling. Four populations of motorcyclists are investigated: Professional (Policemen), Experienced riders, Novices, and Beginners. Method implemented is based of a set of 25 video sequences of driving situations presenting a risk of collision. Participants' task was firstly to stop the video film if they detect a hazard. Then, at the end of each sequence, they have also to assess the criticality of the driving situation as a whole, with a Likert scale (from 0 to 100% of criticality). Results obtained show that cognitive abilities in both (i) hazard detection and (ii) situational criticality assessment depend of the riding experience, and are learnt from two different timing. On one side, Professional and Experienced riders obtained better results than Novices and Beginners for hazard perception (i.e. shortest reaction time). In terms of situational criticality assessment, Beginners underestimate the situational risk and seem overconfident in their abilities to manage the situational risk, against Novices, Professional and Experienced riders, who have better competences in criticality assessment. From these empirical results, a conceptual model of motorcyclists' Risk Awareness is proposed.

NOVICE RIDERS, PRACTICE
Coordination dynamics of the horse-rider system
Lagarde, J., Kelso, J. A., Peham, C., & Licka, T. (January 01, 2005). Coordination dynamics of the horse-rider system. *Journal of Motor Behavior, 37,* 6, 418-24.

The authors studied the interaction between rider and horse by measuring their ensemble motions in a trot sequence, comparing 1 expert and 1 novice rider. Whereas the novice's movements displayed transient departures from phase synchrony, the expert's motions were continuously phase-matched with those of the horse. The tight ensemble synchrony between the expert and the horse was accompanied by an increase in the temporal regularity of the oscillations of the trunk of the horse. Observed differences between expert and novice riders indicated that phase synchronization is by no means perfect but requires extended practice. Points of contact between horse and rider may haptically convey effective communication between them.

EMBODIED COGNITION, MENTAL IMAGERY
Effects of action on children's and adults' mental imagery
Frick, A., Daum, M. M., Wilson, M., & Wilkening, F. (September 01, 2009). Effects of action on children's and adults' mental imagery. *Journal of Experimental Child Psychology, 104,* 1, 34-51.

The aim of this study was to investigate whether and which aspects of a concurrent motor activity can facilitate children's and adults' performance in a dynamic imagery task. Children (5-, 7-, and 9-year-olds) and adults were asked to tilt empty glasses, filled with varied amounts of imaginary water, so that the imagined water would reach the rim. Results showed that in a manual tilting task where glasses could be tilted actively with visual feedback, even 5-year-olds performed well.

Visible embodiment: gestures as simulated action
Hostetter, A. B., & Alibali, M. W. (January 01, 2008). Visible embodiment: gestures as simulated action. *Psychonomic Bulletin & Review, 15,* 3, 495-514.

Spontaneous gestures that accompany speech are related to both verbal and spatial processes. We argue that gestures emerge from perceptual and motor simulations that underlie embodied language and mental imagery. We first review current thinking about embodied cognition, embodied language, and embodied mental imagery. We then provide evidence that gestures stem from spatial representations and mental images. We then propose the gestures-as-simulated-action framework to explain how gestures might arise from an embodied cognitive system. Finally, we compare this framework with other current models of gesture production, and we briefly outline predictions that derive from the framework.

Lingodroids: socially grounding place names in privately grounded cognitive maps

Schulz, R., Wyeth, G., & Wiles, J. (January 01, 2011). Lingodroids: socially grounding place names in privately grounded cognitive maps. *Adaptive Behaviour, 19*, 6, 409-424.

For mobile robots to communicate meaningfully about their spatial environment, they require personally constructed cognitive maps and social interactions to form languages with shared meanings. Geographic spatial concepts introduce particular problems for grounding--connecting a word to its referent in the world--because such concepts cannot be directly and solely based on sensory perceptions. In this article we investigate the grounding of geographic spatial concepts using mobile robots with cognitive maps, called Lingodroids. Languages were established through structured interactions between pairs of robots called where-are-we conversations. The robots used a novel method, termed the distributed lexicon table, to create flexible concepts. This method enabled words for locations, termed toponyms, to be grounded through experience. Their understanding of the meaning of words was demonstrated using go-to games in which the robots independently navigated to named locations. Studies in real and virtual reality worlds show that the system is effective at learning spatial language: robots learn words easily--in a single trial as children do--and the words and their meaning are sufficiently robust for use in real world tasks.

Do We Really Gesture More When It Is More Difficult?

Sassenberg, U., & van, . M. E. (May 01, 2010). Do We Really Gesture More When It Is More Difficult?. *Cognitive Science, 34*, 4, 643-664.

Representational co-speech gestures are generally assumed to be increasingly produced in more difficult compared with easier verbal tasks, as maintained by theories suggesting that gestures arise from processing difficulties during speech production. However, the gestures-as-simulated-action framework proposes that more representational gestures are produced with stronger rather than weaker mental representations that are activated in terms of mental simulation in the embodied cognition framework. We tested these two conflicting assumptions by examining verbal route descriptions that were accompanied by spontaneous directional gestures. Easy descriptions with strong activation were accompanied more often by gestures than difficult descriptions with weak activation. Furthermore, only gesture-speech matches-but not gesture-picture matches-were increasingly produced with difficult lateral directions compared with easy nonlateral directions. We argue that lateral gesture-speech matches underlie stronger activated mental representations in mental imagery. Thus, all results are in line with the gestures-as-simulated-action framework and provide evidence against the view that gestures result from processing difficulties.

Embodied spatial transformations: "Body analogy" for the mental rotation of objects

Amorim, M.-A., Isableu, B., & Jarraya, M. (August 01, 2006). Embodied spatial transformations: "Body analogy" for the mental rotation of objects. *Journal of Experimental Psychology: General, 135,* 3, 327-347.

The cognitive advantage of imagined spatial transformations of the human body over that of more unfamiliar objects (e.g., Shepard-Metzler [S-M] cubes) is an issue for validating motor theories of visual perception. In 6 experiments, the authors show that providing S-M cubes with body characteristics (e.g., by adding a head to S-M cubes to evoke a posture) facilitates the mapping of the cognitive coordinate system of one's body onto the abstract shape. In turn, this spatial embodiment improves object shape matching. Thanks to the increased cohesiveness of human posture in people's body schema, imagined transformations of the body operate in a less piecemeal fashion as compared with objects (S-M cubes or swing-arm desk lamps) under a similar spatial configuration, provided that the pose can be embodied. If the pose cannot be emulated (covert imitation) by the sensorimotor system, the facilitation due to motoric embodiment will also be disrupted.

Motor Processes in Children's Mental Rotation

Frick, A., Daum, M., Walser, S., & Mast, F. (January 01, 2009). Motor Processes in Children's Mental Rotation. *Journal of Cognition and Development, 10,* 1-2.

Previous studies with adult human participants revealed that motor activities can influence mental rotation of body parts and abstract shapes. In this study, we investigated the influence of a rotational hand movement on mental rotation performance from a developmental perspective. Children at the age of 5, 8, and 11 years and adults performed a mental rotation task while simultaneously rotating their hand (guided by a handle). The direction of the manual rotation was either compatible or incompatible with the direction of the mental rotation. Response times increased with increasing stimulus orientation angles, indicating that participants of all age groups used mental rotation to perform the task. A differential effect of the compatibility of manual rotation and mental rotation was found for 5-year-olds and 8-year-olds, but not for 11-year-olds and adults. The results of this study suggest that the ability to dissociate motor from visual cognitive processes increases with age.

Spatial and Linguistic Aspects of Visual Imagery in Sentence Comprehension

Bergen, B., Lindsay, S., Matlock, T., & Narayanan, S. (January 01, 2008). Spatial and Linguistic Aspects of Visual Imagery in Sentence Comprehension. *Cognitive Science: a Multidisciplinary Journal, 31,* 5, 733-764.

There is mounting evidence that language comprehension involves the activation of mental imagery of the content of utterances (Barsalou, 1999; Bergen, Chang, &; Narayan, 2004; Bergen, Narayan, &; Feldman, 2003; Narayan, Bergen, &; Weinberg, 2004; Richardson, Spivey, McRae, &; Barsalou, 2003; Stanfield &;

Zwaan, 2001; Zwaan, Stanfield, &; Yaxley, 2002). This imagery can have motor or perceptual content. Three main questions about the process remain under-explored, however. First, are lexical associations with perception or motion sufficient to yield mental simulation, or is the integration of lexical semantics into larger structures, like sentences, necessary? Second, what linguistic elements (e.g., verbs, nouns, etc.) trigger mental simulations? Third, how detailed are the visual simulations that are performed? A series of behavioral experiments address these questions, using a visual object categorization task to investigate whether up- or down-related language selectively interferes with visual processing in the same part of the visual field (following Richardson et al., 2003). The results demonstrate that either subject nouns or main verbs can trigger visual imagery, but only when used in literal sentences about real space - metaphorical language does not yield significant effects - which implies that it is the comprehension of the sentence as a whole and not simply lexical associations that yields imagery effects. These studies also show that the evoked imagery contains detail as to the part of the visual field where the described scene would take place.

Putting in the mind versus putting on the green: Expertise, performance time, and the linking of imagery and action

Beilock, S., & Gonso, S. (January 01, 2008). Putting in the mind versus putting on the green: Expertise, performance time, and the linking of imagery and action. *The Quarterly Journal of Experimental Psychology, 61,* 6, 920-932.

Does manipulating the time available to image executing a sensorimotor skill impact subsequent skill execution outcomes in a similar manner as manipulating execution time itself? Novice and skilled golfers performed a series of imaged golf putts followed by a series of actual golf putts under instructions that emphasized either speeded or nonspeeded imaging/putting execution. Novices putted less accurately (i.e., higher putting error score) following either putting or imagery instructions in which speed was stressed. Skilled golfers showed the opposite pattern. Although more time available to execute a skill enhances novice performance, this extra time harms the proceduralized skill of experts. Manipulating either actual execution time or imagined execution time produces this differential impact on novice and skilled performance outcomes. These results are discussed in terms of the functional equivalence between imagery and action and expertise differences in the attentional control structures governing complex sensorimotor skill execution.

Self-organization of cognitive performance

Van, O. G. C., Holden, J. G., & Turvey, M. T. (September 01, 2003). Self-organization of cognitive performance. *Journal of Experimental Psychology: General, 132,* 3, 331-350.

Background noise is the irregular variation across repeated measurements of human performance. Background noise remains after task and treatment effects are minimized. Background noise refers to intrinsic sources of variability, the intrinsic dynamics of mind and body, and the internal workings of a living being. Two experiments demonstrate 1/f scaling (pink noise) in simple reaction times and speeded word naming times, which round out a catalog of laboratory task demonstrations that background noise is pink noise. Ubiquitous pink noise suggests processes of mind and body that change each other's dynamics. Such interaction-dominant dynamics are found in systems that self-organize their behavior. Self-organization provides an unconventional perspective on cognition, but this perspective closely parallels a contemporary interdisciplinary view of living systems.

Compressing perceived distance with remote tool-use: Real, imagined, and remembered

Davoli, C. C., Brockmole, J. R., & Witt, J. K. (February 01, 2012). Compressing perceived distance with remote tool-use: Real, imagined, and remembered. *Journal of Experimental Psychology: Human Perception and Performance, 38*, 1, 80-89.

Reaching for an object with a tool has been shown to cause a compressed perception of space just beyond arm's reach. It is not known, however, whether tools that have distal, detached effects at far distances can cause this same perceptual distortion. We examined this issue in the current study with targets placed up to 30m away. Participants who illuminated targets with a laser pointer or imagined doing so consistently judged the targets to be closer than those who pointed at the targets with a baton. Furthermore, perceptual distortions that arose from tool-use persisted in memory beyond the moment of interaction. These findings indicate that remote interactions can have the same perceptual consequences as physical interactions, and have implications for an action-specific account of perception.

Memory organization of action events and its relationship to memory performance

Koriat, A., & Pearlman-Avnion, S. (September 01, 2003). Memory organization of action events and its relationship to memory performance. *Journal of Experimental Psychology: General, 132*, 3, 435-454.

Previous research yielded inconsistent results regarding the memory organization of self-performed actions. The authors propose that task performance changes the very basis of memory organization. Enactment during study and test (Experiment 1) yielded stronger enactive clustering (based on motor-movement similarities), whereas verbal encoding yielded stronger conceptual clustering (based on semantic-episodic similarities). Enactment enhanced memory quantity and memory accuracy. Both measures increased with enactive clustering under self-performance instructions but with conceptual clustering under verbal instructions. Enactment only during study (Experiment 2) or only during testing (Experiment 3) also enhanced enactive clustering. It is proposed that different conditions affect the relative salience of different types of memory organization and their relative contribution to recall.

The Non-Literal Enactment Effect: Filling in the Blanks

Noice, H., & Noice, T. (January 01, 2007). The Non-Literal Enactment Effect: Filling in the Blanks. *Discourse Processes, 44*, 2, 73-89.

A large body of research has shown that verbal phrases such as "move the pen" are better remembered when they are physically enacted than when the same phrases are studied under standard verbal learning instructions (e.g., Engelkamp & Krumnacker, 1980). More recently, a non-literal enactment effect was discovered in which verbal material that was not literally congruent with the accompanying movement was nevertheless better remembered if the speaker had been moving during the utterance. The early demonstrations of this phenomenon involved actors' performances on stage, but the effects were later replicated with non-actors in a lab. A possible explanation for the non-literal effect is that the words and the performed actions are connected at a goal level. In the preliminary study, self-reports of professional actors revealed that all on-stage movements are carefully designed to explain or constrain how the accompanying verbal material constitutes an attempt to reach a goal. In the main study, it was found that this non-verbal information is sufficiently explicit so that non-actors, unacquainted with the situation or the dialogue, can accurately determine the intended goal-directed meaning. The connections between the non-literal enactment effect and theories of embodied cognition are discussed, along with the relevance of non-literal enactment to studies on gestures and pragmatics.

EMBODIED COGNITION, BODY ORIENTATION
Mental and manual rotation
Wohlschläger, A., & Wohlschläger, A. (April 01, 1998). Mental and manual rotation. *Journal of Experimental Psychology: Human Perception and Performance, 24,* 2, 397-412.

The relation between mental and manual rotation was investigated in 2 experiments. Experiment 1 compared the response times (RTs) of mental rotation about 4 axes in space with the RTs shown in the same task when participants were allowed to reorient the stimuli by means of rotational hand movements. For the 3 Cartesian axes, RT functions were quantitatively indistinguishable. Experiment 2 investigated interference between mental rotation and 4 kinds of simultaneously executed hand movements that did not reorient the stimuli. Interference was observed only when axes of manual and mental rotation coincided in space. Regardless of the hand used, concordant rotational directions facilitated, whereas discordant directions inhibited, mental rotation. The results suggest that mental object rotation and rotatory object manipulation share a common process that is thought to control the dynamics of both imagined and actually performed object reorientation.

EMBODIED COGNITION, PRACTICE
Interpretative phenomenological analysis and embodied, active, situated cognition
Larkin, M., Eatough, V., & Osborn, M. (January 01, 2011). Interpretative phenomenological analysis and embodied, active, situated cognition. *Theory & Psychology, 21,* 3, 318-337.

We describe here some of the developing conversations between "third phase" cognitive science and phenomenological philosophy. Contributors to these conversations treat cognition as an embodied, active, and situated phenomenon. We argue that, despite much promise, proper engagement with the foundational phenomenological concept of a situated, meaning-making person has yet to be fully reflected in these conversations. We note that the outcomes of this dialogue have important implications for the field of phenomenological psychology. In particular, we demonstrate that one qualitative method, interpretative phenomenological analysis, can make a useful contribution to the ongoing developments in this field. We suggest that it can provide a valuable hermeneutic counterpoint to the primacy of empiricist methods. Through reference to sustained examples from research participants' accounts of chronic pain, we show how qualitative phenomenological approaches, such as interpretative phenomenological analysis, can illuminate the importance of situating embodied personal experience in the context of meaning, relationships, and the lived world.

Embodied cognitive geographies
Butcher, S. (January 01, 2012). Embodied cognitive geographies. *Progress in Human Geography, 36,* 1, 90-110.

Recent articles in this journal advocated a cognitive poststructuralism as progress for human geography. This research has two flaws. The first is in the epistemological differences between poststructuralism and cognitive semantics, the field from which the authors were informed on embodied cognition. The second problem arises from the contradictions a cognitive poststructuralism would have to other embodied geographies espousing non-representational theory (NRT). This article details and then resolves these two problems in several discussions and relevant examples involving cognitive semantics, embodied realism, embodiment. The product is a non-contradictory poststructural cognitive semantic perspective that provides a possible future path for NRT.

Kinaesonics: The intertwining relationship of body and sound
Bokowiec, M. A. (February 01, 2006). Kinaesonics: The intertwining relationship of body and sound. *Contemporary Music Review, 25,* 1, 47-57.

The focus of this article is on the sensation of the body beneath the mediated and the unique nature and particular forms of sensation and perceptions prompted by interactive technology with particular reference to kinaesonic gestures. These topics will be discussed from the point of view of practice with specific reference to the artists' work with the Bodycoder system and their 2005 work <i>The Suicided Voice</i>. The article will discuss how on-the-body technology alters a performer's perception and sensation prompting new forms of cross-modal (synesthetic) perception. The nature of the 'intertwining' relationship between the sensual and the sonic, inherent in kinaesonic operations, will be outlined. The article will discuss how the intimacy of on-the-body technology problematizes expression, particularly real-time manipulation. The authors will move on to discuss how the natural movement vocabulary of the body becomes the expressive medium for the generation and manipulation of sound. How flexible protocols and a fluid interface that can be re-configured for each new piece of work allow the artists to put the body at the expressive and contextual centre of the work.

Knowledge in Four Deformation Dimensions
Tywoniak, S. (January 01, 2007). Knowledge in Four Deformation Dimensions.*Organization, 14,* 1, 53-76.

This paper sketches a complexity conceptualization of knowledge. Building from evolutionary theories, it defines knowledge as rules that reduce environmental uncertainty through connections between ideas and facts. Knowledge is conceived as a structure validated through action, a process contextualized in individual experience and a system embedded in social and cultural experience. It exhibits four characteristics of a complex system: it is sensitive to initial conditions, exhibits multiple feedback loops, is non-linear and is recursively symmetrical. Knowledge's four interdependent deformation dimensions are identified (personal, common, tacit and explicit) and their interactions are discussed. This conceptualization of knowledge as a complex system contributes to the knowledge-based theory of the firm by providing some micro-foundations to organizational knowledge, and it opens the opportunity to re-think theories of communities of practice, entrepreneurship and firm creation, the role of managers, and knowledge management.

Enhancing spatial ability through sport practice: Evidence for an effect of motor training on mental rotation performance

Moreau, D., Clerc, J., Mansy-Dannay, A., & Guerrien, A. (January 01, 2012). Enhancing spatial ability through sport practice: Evidence for an effect of motor training on mental rotation performance. *Journal of Individual Differences, 33*, 2, 83-88.

This experiment investigated the relationship between mental rotation and sport training. Undergraduate university students (n = 62) completed the Mental Rotation Test (Vandenberg & Kuse, 1978), before and after a 10-month training in two different sports, which either involved extensive mental rotation ability (wrestling group) or did not (running group). Both groups showed comparable results in the pretest, but the wrestling group outperformed the running group in the posttest. As expected from previous studies, males outperformed women in the pretest and the posttest. Besides, self-reported data gathered after both sessions indicated an increase in adaptive strategies following training in wrestling, but not subsequent to training in running. These findings demonstrate the significant effect of training in particular sports on mental rotation performance, thus showing consistency with the notion of cognitive plasticity induced from motor training involving manipulation of spatial representations. They are discussed within an embodied cognition framework.

SITUATED COGNITION, WAYFINDING
Where Am I? How Can I Get There? Impact of Navigability and Narrative Transportation on Spatial Presence

Balakrishnan, B., & Sundar, S. S. (January 01, 2011). Where Am I? How Can I Get There? Impact of Navigability and Narrative Transportation on Spatial Presence. *Human-computer Interaction, 26*, 3, 161-204.

From video games to virtual worlds on the World Wide Web, modern media are becoming increasingly spatial, with users traversing artificial spaces and experiencing a kind of immersion known as "spatial presence." But how do these media induce spatial presence? Are the affordances for movement provided by these technologies responsible for this illusion? Or do narratives that accompany them persuade us to suspend disbelief and transport ourselves into a virtual space? We explore these theoretical questions by pitting the navigability affordances of a video game against narrative transportation and examining their relative contributions to the formation of spatial presence in a virtual reality context. Results from a large experiment (N = 240) reveal that the narrative actually detracts from spatial presence while traversibility (in the form of greater degrees of steering motion) enhances it even without invoking a mental model of the portrayed environment. Theoretical and practical implications are discussed.

SITUATED COGNITION, BODY ORIENTATION
Gestures: Their Role in Teaching and Learning
Roth, W.-M. (January 01, 2001). Gestures: Their Role in Teaching and Learning. *Review of Educational Research, 71,* 3, 365-392.

Gestures are central to human cognition and constitute a pervasive element of human communication across cultures; even congenitally blind individuals use gestures when they talk. Yet there exists virtually no educational research that focuses on the role of gestures in knowing and learning and the implications they have for designing and evaluating learning environments. The purpose of this article is to provide a review of the existing literature in anthropology, linguistics, psychology, and education and, in the context of several concrete analyses of gesture use, to articulate potential focus questions that are relevant to educational research of knowing, learning, and teaching.

SITUATED COGNITION, PRACTICE
Situated Cognition and Communities of Practice: First-Person "Lived Experiences" vs. Third-Person Perspectives
Hung, D., Looi, C.-K., & Koh, T.-S. (January 01, 2004). Situated Cognition and Communities of Practice: First-Person "Lived Experiences" vs. Third-Person Perspectives. *Educational Technology & Society, 7,* 4, 193-200.

This paper considers the work of Martin Heidegger and its relation to situated cognition. The motivation for the paper springs from the perceived misconception that many educators have on situated cognition by applying situated learning strategies in a dualistic orientation, whereas situated cognition is fundamentally relativist (non-dualistic) in epistemology. Hence, we felt that the foundations of situated cognition have to be revisited. In the paper, we relate Heidegger's work to the resurgence of interest in communities of practice and the notions of identity or learning to be (vis-a-vis learning about). We then draw implications to situated cognition and the complementary role of descriptions or representations to situated learning.

Real World Use of Scientific Concepts: Integrating Situated Cognition with Explicit Instruction
Gersten, R., & Baker, S. (December 07, 1998). Real World Use of Scientific Concepts: Integrating Situated Cognition with Explicit Instruction. *Exceptional Children, 65,* 1, 23-35.

Presents a conceptual framework for teaching science to students with disabilities. The framework suggests integration of explicit instruction in critical concepts, with cognitively-based approaches that emphasize problem-solving skills on real-world tasks. Implications for policy, professional development, and creation of learning environments that promote retention and transfer are discussed.

Cognitive and Situated Learning Perspectives in Theory and Practice

An exploration of Mental Imagery

Cobb, P., & Bowers, J. (January 01, 1999). Cognitive and Situated Learning Perspectives in Theory and Practice. *Educational Researcher, 28,* 2, 4-15.

In their recent exchange, Anderson, Reder, and Simon (1996 Anderson, Reder, and Simon (1997) and Greeno (1997) frame the conflicts between cognitive theory and situated learning theory in terms of issues that are primarily of interest to educational psychologists. We attempt to broaden the debate by approaching this discussion of perspectives against the background of our concerns as educators who engage in classroom-based research and instructional design in collaboration with teachers. We first delineate the underlying differences between the two perspectives by distinguishing their central organizing metaphors. We then argue that the contrast between the two perspectives cannot be reduced to that of choosing between the individual and the social collective as the primary unit of analysis. Against this background, we compare the situated viewpoint we find useful in our work with the cognitive approach advocated by Anderson et al. by focusing on their treatments of meaning and instructional goals. Finally, we consider the potential contributions of the two perspectives to instructional practice by contrasting their differing formulations of the relationship between theory and practice.

Mental Imagery in Air Traffic Control

Shorrock, S., & Isaac, A. (January 01, 2010). Mental Imagery in Air Traffic Control. *The International Journal of Aviation Psychology, 20,* 4, 309-324.

Mental imagery is known to play a significant role in the skilled performance of complex cognitive tasks, yet is mostly overlooked in the field of air traffic control-a task that is reliant on what controllers term "the picture." This article explores 3 strands of imagery research: the similarities between imagery and perception, individual differences in imagery, and skill learning and imagery. The research reported is discussed in terms of fundamental implications for air traffic control, implications for the measurement of imagery, implications for training, and implications for technology design.

COGNITIVE ERGONOMICS, WAYFINDING

The railway as a socio-technical system: human factors at the heart of successful rail engineering

Wilson, J. R., Farrington-Darby, T., Cox, G., Bye, R., & Hockey, G. R. J. (January 01, 2007). The railway as a socio-technical system: human factors at the heart of successful rail engineering. *Proceedings of the Institution of Mechanical Engineers, Part F: Journal of Rail and Rapid Transit, 221,* 1, 101-115.

High-quality engineering and operations management are key to meeting all the requirements of a successful railway-quality of service, reliable and safe performance, and maximum possible use of capacity. However, the railway is a socio-technical system and therefore has human factors at its core, which requires a strong integrated ergonomics contribution. Moreover, this contribution must be at a systems level rather than providing point solutions to particular equipment, interface, workplace, or job problems. This paper draws from the first two human factors projects in the EPSRC Rail Research UK programme, interpreting them for an engineering audience. The paper first emphasizes and gives examples of the need for a systems ergonomics contribution to engineering an improved railway. Then the available literature is summarized in a structured fashion. Finally, a short summary is provided of the research which has started to develop a distributed cognition model of work on the railways, especially across functional groups of signalling, control, and train driving.

COGNITIVE ERGONOMICS, BODY ORIENTATION
Effects of tactile cueing on concurrent performance of military and robotics tasks in a simulated multitasking environment
Chen, J. Y. C., & Terrence, P. I. (January 01, 2008). Effects of tactile cueing on concurrent performance of military and robotics tasks in a simulated multitasking environment. *Ergonomics, 51,* 8, 1137-1152.

This study examined the concurrent performance of military gunnery, robotics control and communication tasks in a simulated environment. More specifically, the study investigated how aided target recognition (AiTR) capabilities (delivered either through tactile or tactile+visual cueing) for the gunnery task might benefit overall performance. Results showed that AiTR benefited not only the gunnery task, but also the concurrent robotics and communication tasks. The participants' spatial ability was found to be a good indicator of their gunnery and robotics task performance. However, when AiTR was available to assist their gunnery task, those participants of lower spatial ability were able to perform their robotics tasks as well as those of higher spatial ability. Finally, participants' workload assessment was significantly higher when they teleoperated (i.e. remotely operated) a robot and when their gunnery task was unassisted. These results will further understanding of multitasking performance in military tasking environments. These results will also facilitate the implementation of robots in military settings and will provide useful data to military system designs.

COGNITIVE ERGONOMICS, PRACTICE
Does Team Training Improve Team Performance? A Meta-Analysis
Salas, E., DiazGranados, D., Klein, C., Burke, C., Stagl, K., Goodwin, G., & Halpin, S. (January 01, 2008). Does Team Training Improve Team Performance? A Meta-Analysis. *Human Factors, 50,* 6, 903-933.

Objective: This research effort leveraged the science of training to guide a taxonomic integration and a series of meta-analyses to gauge the effectiveness and boundary conditions of team training interventions for enhancing team outcomes. Background: Disparate effect sizes across primary studies have made it difficult to determine the true strength of the relationships between team training techniques and team outcomes. Method: Several meta-analytic integrations were conducted to examine the relationships between team training interventions and team functioning. Specifically, we assessed the relative effectiveness of these interventions on team cognitive, affective, process, and performance outcomes. Training content, team membership stability, and team size were investigated as potential moderators of the relationship between team training and outcomes. In total, the database consisted of 93 effect sizes representing 2,650 teams. Results: The results suggested that moderate, positive relationships exist between team training interventions and each of the outcome types. The findings of moderator analyses indicated that training content, team membership stability, and team size moderate the effectiveness of these interventions. Conclusion: Our findings suggest that team training interventions are a viable approach organizations can take in order to enhance team outcomes. They are useful for improving cognitive outcomes, affective outcomes, teamwork processes, and performance outcomes. Moreover, results suggest that training content, team membership stability, and team size moderate the effectiveness of team training interventions. Application: Applications of the results from this research are numerous. Those who design and administer training can benefit from these findings in order to improve the effectiveness of their team training interventions.

SEMIOTICS, WAYFINDING
The Arrow--Directional Semiotics: Wayfinding in Transit
Fuller, G. (January 01, 2002). The Arrow--Directional Semiotics: Wayfinding in Transit.*Social Semiotics, 12,* 3, 231-244.

Airport language is a spectacle, an interface for social relations between humans and machines. Signage intensifies social relations--reconfiguring territories of geophysical/architectural space into territories of recognition that speak to a productive power of language that is fundamentally non-representational. Airports are walked, the signs don't accompany or reflect upon the airport, they are machined into it. The traveller navigates through a highly textually mediated space where the signs not only enact semioticised territories but also directly intervene into the material machinic processes of travelling. As Guattari (1992: 49) might say, these point-signs 'don't simply secrete significations'. They activate the bringing into being of ontological universes. This paper focuses on 'signage' in a quite expanded yet also limited sense. It focuses on the increasing standardisation of the signifying semiologies of transit wayfinding systems which signal the primacy of pragmatic interactivity in the communicative event of

walking the airport. If the controlling semiosis of non-places is, as Auge (1995) notes, the dominant space of supermodernity, then a thorough consideration of such signifying technologies would seem in order. This paper focuses on one of the most ubiquitous signs at the airport: the arrow. The airport's arrow is an asemic figure through which perhaps to read the semiotic technologies of the airport itself. The arrow is both a tool and a trope for the imperatives of global transit: it turns place into passage, striates space into controlled flows, and urges the traveller to 'move on'. It is a point sign that leads the way to a consideration of the technologies, both semiotic and a-semiotic, that provide the navigational and behavioural guidance that is increasingly in evidence, not only at the airport but in all public spaces.

Placing subway signs: practical properties of signs at work
Denis, J., & Pontille, D. (January 01, 2010). Placing subway signs: practical properties of signs at work. *Visual Communication, 9,* 4, 441-462.

This article complements previous studies stressing the importance of the emplacement of signs in public spaces by focusing on the placement process itself. The authors' ethnographic study of the Paris subway shows that the way-finding system operates in a process of graphical ordering within which the standardized shape, content and emplacement of each sign are crucial. However, the placement work does not simply consist of following instructions. The authors show that, in order to find the proper place for boards, stickers and posters, workers have to explore the environment and reconcile the sign placement policy with the ecology of the local sites. In doing so, workers do not just discover an emplacement designated for a particular sign but enact an available place, mobilizing numerous embodied practices. During this process, signs themselves are not treated as stabilized entities; they oscillate between what the authors term 'practical properties' that arise from the combination of objects, bodies and environment.

SEMIOTICS, PRACTICE
Semiotics of space: Peirce and Lefebvre
Mèaèattèanen, P. (January 01, 2007). Semiotics of space: Peirce and Lefebvre.*Semiotica, 2007*, 166, 453-461.

Henri Lefebvre discusses the problem of a spatial code for reading, interpreting, and producing the space we live in. He is not content with the linguistic approach where the notion of meaning is defined in terms of language. The semiotic theory of Charles Peirce provides the required elements for this kind of spatial code. Meaning is defined as a habit of action, and this notion of meaning can be applied not only to linguistic expressions but also to things like hats, tables, buildings, and squares. In other words, meaning is defined as use - use of objects and instruments, our own organic body included. This wider notion of meaning provides the required semiotics of space.

TRAIL DESIGN, PRACTICE
Profiling Australian Snowsport Injuries: A Snapshot from the Snowy Mountains
Dickson, T., Gray, T., Downey, G., Saunders, J., & Newman, C. (January 01, 2008). Profiling Australian Snowsport Injuries: A Snapshot from the Snowy Mountains. *Journal of Sport &; Tourism, 13*, 4, 273-295.

Snowsport tourism provides a major economic contribution to the rural and regional areas surrounding the major resorts in Australia. One of the barriers to snowsport participation is that people perceive snowsports as dangerous and so fear being injured. Understanding snowsport injuries will help managers to diminish the risk of injuries, and marketers to address perceptions of danger. This study explored snowsport-related injuries to participants aged 18 years and older in the Snowy Mountains, Australia, over 31 days during winter 2006. Of 497 injured snowsport participants surveyed, 76.3% were visiting the area for a holiday, while 16.9% were working in the area for the snow season; 45% were women, 55% were men; 33.2% were aged 18-24 years; with 49.3% being alpine skiers and 46.1% snowboarders. For skiers the main injury was to the knee (75.6%), while for snowboarders the wrist was the main injury location (84.6%). The primary location where injuries occurred was on piste at the resort (47.5%) with the main mechanism of injury being falling over (38.2%). Most injuries, as reported by the respondents, were either bruises or sprains (72%). Most people did not wear any protective equipment while participating (73.2%). Of the two main activity groups, skiers had the highest proportion who did not wear any protective equipment (78.8%) while snowboarders were most likely to wear helmets (18.8%). Results from this study will be useful to inform future snowsport safety messages and strategies that target various factors that may contribute to snowsport injuries including behaviours and attitudes before and during participation.

PARK DESIGN, PRACTICE
Skatepark as Neoliberal Playground
Howell, O. (January 01, 2008). Skatepark as Neoliberal Playground. *Space and Culture,11*, 4, 475-496.

More than 2,000 skateboard parks have been built in the United States over the past decade. Although these parks are a response to community demand, many cities have provided these facilities on certain neoliberal conditions. As a review of parks management literature reveals, cities assume no liability for injuries and expect skateboarders to secure private funding; urban managers also expect skateboarders to display character traits of personal responsibility and entrepreneurial-ism. This is in contrast to Progressive Era playgrounds, where cities completely financed playgrounds and took responsibility for personal safety; urban managers also sought to inculcate values of loyalty, which they viewed as necessary in an increasingly bureaucratized society. The comparison highlights how the skatepark can be viewed as an instance in which neoliberal governance practices have reconfigured the citizen—state relationship from one of entitlement to one of contractualism.

Locating Skateparks: The Planner's Dilemma
Freeman, C., & Riordan, T. (August 01, 2002). Locating Skateparks: The Planner's Dilemma. *Planning Practice and Research, 17*, 3, 297-316.

Skateboarding and use of open public space

OBSTACLES, MENTAL IMAGERY
Perspectives on prediction: Does third-person imagery improve task completion estimates?
Buehler, R., Griffin, D., Lam, K. C. H., & Deslauriers, J. (January 01, 2012). Perspectives on prediction: Does third-person imagery improve task completion estimates?.*Organizational Behavior and Human Decision Processes, 117*, 1, 138-149.

People typically underestimate the time necessary to complete their tasks. According to the planning fallacy model of optimistic time predictions, this underestimation occurs because people focus on developing a specific plan for the current task and neglect the implications of past failures to meet similar deadlines. We extend the classic planning fallacy model by proposing that a phenomenal quality of mental imagery - the visual perspective that is adopted - may moderate the optimistic prediction bias. Consistent with this proposal, participants in four studies predicted longer completion times, and thus were less prone to bias, when they imagined an upcoming task from the third-person rather than first-person perspective. Third-person imagery reduced people's focus on optimistic plans, increased their focus on potential obstacles, and decreased the impact of task-relevant motives on prediction. The findings suggest that third-person imagery helps individuals generate more realistic predictions by reducing cognitive and motivational processes that typically contribute to bias.

OBSTACLES, WAYFINDING

Perceiving curvilinear heading in the presence of moving objects

Fajen, B. R., & Kim, N.-G. (October 01, 2002). Perceiving curvilinear heading in the presence of moving objects. *Journal of Experimental Psychology: Human Perception and Performance, 28,* 5, 1100-1119.

Four experiments were directed at understanding the influence of multiple moving objects on curvilinear (i.e., circular and elliptical) heading perception. Displays simulated observer movement over a ground plane in the presence of moving objects depicted as transparent, opaque, or black cubes. Objects either moved parallel to or intersected the observer's path and either retreated from or approached the moving observer. Heading judgments were accurate and consistent across all conditions. The significance of these results for computational models of heading perception and for information in the global optic flow field about observer and object motion is discussed.

Environmental topography and postural control demands shape aging-associated decrements in spatial navigation performance

Lövdén, M., Schellenbach, M., Grossman-Hutter, B., Krüger, A., & Lindenberger, U. (December 01, 2005). Environmental topography and postural control demands shape aging-associated decrements in spatial navigation performance. *Psychology and Aging,20,* 4, 683-694.

This study tests the hypothesis that aging-induced cognitive permeation of sensorimotor functions contributes to adult age differences in spatial navigation performance. Virtual maze-like museums were projected in front of a treadmill. Sixteen 20-30-year-old men and sixteen 60-70-year-old men performed a way-finding task in city-block or variable topographies while walking with or without support. Walking support attenuated age-related decrements in navigational learning. Navigation load increased trunk-angle variability for older adults only. Age differences in spatial knowledge persisted despite perfect place-finding performance. City-block topography was easier than variable topography for younger adults only, indicating age-related differences in reliance on spatial relational learning. Attempts at supporting older adults' navigation performance should consider sensorimotor/cognitive interactions and qualitative differences in navigational activity.

Perceiving motion while moving: How pairwise nominal invariants make optical flow cohere

Cutting, J. E., & Readinger, W. O. (June 01, 2002). Perceiving motion while moving: How pairwise nominal invariants make optical flow cohere. *Journal of Experimental Psychology: Human Perception and Performance, 28,* 3, 731-747.

Computer-generated sequences simulated observer movement toward 10 randomly placed poles, 1 moving and 9 stationary. When observers judged their direction of movement, or heading, they used 3 related invariants: The (a) convergence and (b) decelerating divergence of any 2 poles specified that heading was to the outside of the nearer pole, and the (c) crossover of 2 poles specified that heading was to the outside of the farther pole. With all poles stationary, the field of 45 pairwise movements yielded a coherent specification of heading. With 1 pole moving with respect to the others, however, the field a could yield an incoherent heading solution. Such incoherence was readily detectable; similar pole motion leading to coherent flow, however, was less readily detectable.

OBSTACLES, BODY ORIENTATION

Judging beforehand the possibility of passing under obstacles without motion: the influence of egocentric and geocentric frames of reference

Bringoux, L., Robic, G., Gauthier, G., & Vercher, J. (January 01, 2008). Judging beforehand the possibility of passing under obstacles without motion: the influence of egocentric and geocentric frames of reference. *Experimental Brain Research, 185,* 4, 673-680.

Previous studies have shown that the perception of the earth-based visual horizon, also named Gravity Referenced Eye Level (GREL), is modified by body tilt around a trans-ocular axis. Here, we investigated whether estimates of the elevation of a luminous horizontal line presented on a screen in otherwise darkness and estimates of the possibility of passing under are identically related to body tilt in absence of motion. Results showed that subjects overestimated the elevation of the projected line, whatever their body orientation. In the same way, subjects also overestimated their capacity of passing under the line. Both estimates appeared as a linear function of body tilt, that is, forward body tilt yielded increased overestimations, and backward body tilt yielded decreased overestimations. More strikingly, the linear effect of body tilt upon these estimates is comparable to that previously observed for direct GREL judgements. Overall, these data strongly suggest that the perception of the elevation of a visible obstacle and the perception of the ability of passing under in otherwise darkness shared common processes which are intimately linked to the GREL perception. The effect of body tilt upon these perceptions may illustrate an egocentric influence upon the semi-geocentric frame of reference required to perform the task. Possible interactions between egocentric and geocentric frames of reference are discussed.

Influence of gaze elevation on estimating the possibility of passing under high obstacles during body tilt

Bourrelly, A., Bringoux, L., & Vercher, J.-L. (January 01, 2009). Influence of gaze elevation on estimating the possibility of passing under high obstacles during body tilt.*Experimental Brain Research, 193,* 1, 19-28.

We investigated the influence of gaze elevation on judging the possibility of passing under high obstacles during pitch body tilts, while stationary, in absence of allocentric cues. Specifically, we aimed at studying the influence of egocentric references upon geocentric judgements. Seated subjects, orientated at various body orientations, were asked to perceptually estimate the possibility of passing under a projected horizontal line while keeping their gaze on a fixation target and imagining a horizontal body displacement. The results showed a global overestimation of the possibility of passing under the line, and confirmed the influence of body orientation reported by Bringoux et al. (Exp Brain Res 185(4):673-680, 2008). More strikingly, a linear influence of gaze elevation was found on perceptual estimates. Precisely, downward eye elevation yielded increased overestimations, and conversely upward gaze elevation yielded decreased overestimations. Furthermore, body and gaze orientation effects were independent and combined additively to yield a global egocentric influence with a weight of 45 and 54%, respectively. Overall, our data suggest that multiple egocentric references can jointly affect the estimated possibility of passing under high obstacles. These results are discussed in terms of "interpenetrability" between geocentric and egocentric reference frames and clearly demonstrate that gaze elevation is involved, as body orientation, in geocentric spatial localization.

Perception-Movement Coupling in the Regulation of Step Lengths When Approaching an Obstacle

Cornus, S., Laurent, M., & Laborie, S. (January 01, 2009). Perception-Movement Coupling in the Regulation of Step Lengths When Approaching an Obstacle. *Ecological Psychology, 21*, 4, 334-367.

Experiment 1 showed that the control mechanism based on a perception-movement coupling observed in certain goal-directed movement tasks (De Rugy, Montagne, Buekers, & Laurent, 2000; Montagne, Cornus, Glize, Quaine, & Laurent, 2000) can be extended to a stepping across an obstacle task. Regardless of the specificity of tasks, the initiation of regulations is a function of the amount of adjustment. Our participants organized their regulation later than long jumpers. Two additional experiments were conceived to investigate whether this control mechanism could be generalized to goal-directed locomotor displacements, with different constraints. The aim of Experiments 2 and 3 was to address the adaptation of this control mechanism by manipulating the obstacle width and the walking speed in a stepping across task. The results showed that the functioning of this control mechanism could be influenced by the spatiotemporal constraints. Participants' behavior depended on a perception-movement coupling. This study suggests the existence of a generic control mechanism based on a perception-movement coupling, and it emphasizes the adaptation of this type of control mechanism involved in goal-directed displacements.

MENTAL IMAGERY, SKILL PROGRESSION
The conceptual process of skill progression development in artistic gymnastics

Irwin, G., Hanton, S., & Kerwin, D. (January 01, 2005). The conceptual process of skill progression development in artistic gymnastics. *Journal of Sports Sciences, 23*, 10, 1089-1099.

In this study, we examined the methods used and knowledge required by 16 elite men's gymnastic coaches in the development of skill progressions. Following in-depth interviews, a conceptual model representing the process of skill progression development was generated. We found that: (1) elite gymnastic coaches developed skill progressions through experimental practice, reflection and critical inquiry; (2) the development of skill progressions was underpinned by the coaches acquiring a mindset based on four further sub-components (i.e. skill progression refinement, current coaching knowledge, mental imagery and biomechanical understanding); and (3) coaches identified the importance of replication of the spatial and temporal characteristics of the final skill. The results are consistent with task analysis, reflective practice and the principle of specificity. Practically, these findings suggest the need to develop coaches with a more objective approach to skill progression development and a greater understanding of the controlling mechanisms inherent in such practices.

An exploration of Mental Imagery

ABOUT THE AUTHOR

Benjamin is a connoisseur of learning and performance.

He has maintained certification as a Certified Strength and Condition Specialist and an NSCA Certified Personal Trainer for nearly seven years.

He holds master of science degrees in Human Centered Design and Engineering from the University of Washington and in Quality Management from Mountain State University, and bachelors of science degrees in Mechanical and Aerospace Engineering from West Virginia University.

He is an ATP rated helicopter pilot, holds a commercial pilot rating in single and multiengine airplanes, and is a Certified Flight Instructor (Instrument) in helicopters and airplanes. He also is a rated NVG helicopter pilot and instructor with over 1500 hours of flight time.

Benjamin also served an enlistment with the Army National Guard's 19th Special Forces Group (Airborne) in support of the Global War on Terrorism.

Made in the USA
Coppell, TX
23 January 2020